Mastery-Based Learning in Mathematics (K-8)
Instructional Model (IM^3)

Jack Hunter & Abbey Mezinko

MASTERY BASED LEARNING IN MATHEMATICS (K-8)
Instructional Model IM3

J. Hunter Venture Group

If you are interested in learning more about Mastery-Based Learning please contact Jack and Abbey at: **contact@jhunterventuregroup.com**
Follow Jack on Twitter at: @ Principaljack
www.jhunterventuregroup.com
Also look for Hunter's other publications available on the website.

Copyright © 2018 by Jack Hunter & Abbey Mezinko
Printed in the United States of America

ISBN 978-0692162309

J Hunter Venture Group, LLC Publishing

All rights reserved. This book or any portion thereof
may not be reproduced or used in any manner whatsoever without the
express written permission of the publisher except for the use of brief
quotations in a book review.

First Edition 10 9 8 7 6 5 4 3 2 1

Jack dedicates to:
My children Max and Lilly, my wife Beth, and my mother Cherie,
for encouraging me to leave a legacy for all educators.

Abbey dedicates to:
My husband Sam, my son Max and my aunt Linda,
for all of the support while I completed this mission.

Table of Contents

Introduction

Chapter One: Challenge the Status Quo………………….......9

Chapter Two: The New Vision……………..……………….17

Chapter Three: Support from the Instructional Leader….....43

Chapter Four: Preparing the Vision……………….……..…62

Chapter Five: Implement in the Classroom………..………..71

Chapter Six: Motivating the Learners……………….…..…..80

Chapter Seven: Getting Staff to Buy In……………….…...105

Chapter Eight: The Evidence………………………….…....118

Summary……………………………………………….……126

Author Background……………………………………...…127

Sample Mastery Problems………………………………….131

Introduction

*"You cannot be anything you want to be -
but you can be a lot more of who you already are."*
Don Clifton

In Daniel Pink's bestselling book *Drive* he states "Control leads to compliance; autonomy leads to engagement." As I looked around the school I saw some classrooms full of compliant learners who were not engaged and found few classrooms where learners were engaged and academically compliant. Academically *compliant* meant they were on task, not students sitting as if they were robots on an assembly line such as "listen, memorize, regurgitate and forget."

As I began to look at my current organization, under the adage that control leads to compliance, a few glaring observations struck me. Realizing I had a school with tremendous potential and a large portion of educators looking for direction, I knew I could devise a way to engage learners and also increase their aptitude. Pink goes on to state the ingredients of genuine motivation are autonomy, mastery and purpose. This became the mantra of the instructional model of mastery in mathematics initiative, IM^3 that I was intending on introducing to my current school. Pink states "Studies in behavioral science states autonomous motivation promotes greater conceptual understanding, better grades and enhanced persistence at school." This was exactly what my school needed and what I intended to deliver.

You will acquire strategies, learn about what high performing math mastery instruction looks like, as well as view examples of various levels of math problems used in this instructional model IM^3. In Gary Keller's book *The One Thing,* he discussed what occurs on World Domino Day in the Netherlands. On this day in 2009, Domino Productions lined up 4,491,863 dominoes and when a single domino went in motion, it unleashed more than 94,000 joules of energy. That is the same amount it takes for an average male to do 545 pushups. Each domino represented a small amount of potential energy.

I tell that story to educators and students when I discuss why it is important to develop mastery in mathematics; believing that one domino (standard) can create enough energy for you to learn all the significant standards for you to be successful. Almost all kids understand dominos and seem to relate well to the above example. When we show students through formative feedback how well they are progressing and how many standards they are mastering, we can use this analogy of creating energy that can continue with effort. This instructional model of math mastery-based initiative IM^3 has proven to be successful and you will see how you can apply this to your classroom or school.

"Are you ready to start your Instructional Journey to Mastery Island?"

Chapter One

Dare to Challenge the Status Quo

"Discontent with the Status Quo is a Great Catalyst for Vision"
John Maxwell

As I was completing my fifth year as principal at my current school, I began looking for ways I could advance educators in my building to make a more significant impact on student growth. I have attended extensive professional learning opportunities and have gained incredible insight into all aspects of pedagogy and application. I recently attended in 2018, a professional learning at MIT in Boston on how to incorporate computer science in mathematics. I knew that our students and educators needed assistance finding strategies that improved student growth. We were improving above the norm in our district and the state. While the growth was satisfying, we were far behind the state math average and we needed something innovative to motivate our staff to make a significant difference in the lives of every student. I first attended a John Hattie conference on his meta-analysis studies in 2016, which created the inspiration I needed to increase our math scores more than the norm we were currently achieving. I attended another Hattie conference in 2017, and again in 2018, and became fluent in his evidence-based practices. When applied correctly, evidence-based practices in mathematics will enhance student performance and growth. I knew that Hattie's evidence-based strategies could impact instruction at my current school with the right structures. **See the vignette**

at the end of the chapter for a look on how I created a learning opportunity for my staff through Hattie's work.

I had heard of Mastery-Based learning but wanted to create a hybrid between personalized learning and individualization. I was familiar with both frameworks and found some of the instructional frameworks applicable to urban education. Creating a mix of personalized learning and individualization while encompassing an intrinsic motivation system led us to develop the framework we will be discussing. The main commonality that resonated with me about all the frameworks was the focus on each individual student and his or her abilities.

I was ready to challenge the status quo!

In our district, if you gained 7% growth in a year, you were deemed effective. Having students who were two to three grade levels behind in mathematics and moving 7% growth did nothing to change the culture of the school or the school community. It was my responsibility as the Lead Learner or Instructional Leader to lead the implementation of Mastery Based Learning in mathematics using this instructional model IM^3 we created. After learning about all the evidence-based practices from Hattie and other professional education researchers, I was ready for full implementation into the school.

As I broke down the school-wide state summative math data, I began to see, as a school, we were not meeting the needs of every student. I found some glaring gaps. The learners, who came into Kindergarten on grade level in math, remained at the correct grade level throughout their career in most instances. However, about 28% of our school population is transient. So, as I was looking at the data, I only found three students who were registered at my school for the duration of Kindergarten through their 8th grade year. The lack of continuous enrollment made the data collection more variable and unpredictable. The data included students who transferred into my school which accounted for a portion of our below-level learners. Students in our school are from a disadvantaged background and all receive 100% free lunch. Although our school is a STEMM Academy, our student population is representative of the neighborhood where the school is located. We do not interview students for acceptance to our school. If they live within the district boundaries of our school, they can attend. We struggle with a chronic absenteeism rate of over 20%. The absenteeism rate is one of the highest in the district and became a condition I needed to improve in order to approach this Mastery-Based initiative IM³ in mathematics. In Chapter Three, I will provide details of what systems I used to mitigate the high absenteeism rate.

The traditional mathematics instruction we were providing our learners was working, however not fast enough and not on a scalable basis. We were still educating all the kids one way, in the traditional fashion and differentiating some of the time.

This is where the journey begins, mastery classrooms become successful and the change begins! Using this Instructional Model in Mathematics IM³

Choosing to Challenge the Status Quo

As I mentioned previously, I was viewed as an excellent administrator focusing on instructional leadership. I received the Principal of the Year award in my second year and was nominated again in my fifth year. I was featured in newspaper articles, videos, the local news and other forms of media. The acknowledgment was all very flattering, however, I needed to continue to be laser focused on student achievement and improve the state appraisal of my current school. I first had to make sure the culture was a positive, safe environment for learning and that I could get the right teachers "on board the ship". I would like to say this only took a few months, however, it took closer to a year to get all staff members to see the positive changes that were planned. We developed mission and vision statements, which also created more positive changes. I used Anthony Muhammad's quote with my staff and we began as a group to break down what we needed to do together to move our school forward: "School culture is like soil and climate is like a seed. If the soil is healthy the seed will grow, if the soil is toxic the seed will die." One example of a non – productive classroom strategy I observed was students playing non-academic games and other non-instructional items in some classrooms when I was conducting classroom walkthroughs. I also observed a percentage of educators teaching by completing worksheets with their students.

This new cultural accountability started a change as I challenged the status quo. The focus on culture and climate was starting to show positive changes in the classrooms. I needed, as an instructional leader, to begin looking at ways to improve student performance and growth. When we compared our school's previous data to schools of similar demographics, we looked excellent on paper. We used the following demographics when comparing: free/reduced lunch, attendance percentage, transiency rate and enrollment.

Leading the Change of the Status Quo

As a principal, it is imperative that you are viewed as an Instructional Leader or Lead Learner in your organization. Principals' roles have expanded over the past few decades with the advent of school and teacher accountability. Even in the past four years, I have noticed the increased accountability on leadership at the school level. Although success should not be about achievement on standardized tests, in the current educational landscape, much attention is paid to that metric of student achievement. In any organization, strength of content or product must start at the very top. It was believed in recent years and through Hattie's research, that principals had little impact on student achievement (.12 effect size). However, as more research is compiled, from John Hattie and Viviane Robinson , for example, research shows there are various ways leaders can enhance student growth through their practice. This effect size research was essential to ensure I was leading the initiative with the correct research. Effect size is a simple way of quantifying the difference between two groups that has many advantages over the use of typical tests of statistical significance alone. The calculation of the effect size is actually quite simple and is the standardized mean difference between the two groups. If the leader of an organization does not have buy-in for the initiative, it simply won't work.

Here is some of the current research from 2008 and beyond that shows how crucial instructional leadership is to an organization.

Viviane Robinson Effect Size of Educational Leadership Research:

1. Establishing Goals and Expectations (.42)
2. Resourcing Strategically (.31)
3. Ensuring Quality Teaching (.42)
4. Leading Teacher Learning and Development (.84)
5. Ensuring an Orderly and Safe Environment (.27)

Hattie's New Research

Leaders who see their primary role as to evaluate their impact can yield an effect size of .91. Evaluating their own impact ensures that self-reflection, continued learning and integration into the school culture occurs. I knew I had the ambition and skill to move this new initiative of mastery in mathematics. Through daily self-reflection, professional learning and providing evidence-based strategies and feedback to educators, this effect size of .91 was within reach.

The above-listed Hattie practice reiterates the fact that leadership does matter in education. It is not satisfactory to just "run" a building anymore. As a leader, you must continually evaluate yourself and the practices that your educators are using to instruct the children in your school. Your role is to facilitate conversations and provide resources for all educators to use the best strategies, allowing students to reach math mastery with the greatest level of efficiency possible.

Calculating My Effect Size

I was now ready to calculate and evaluate my own effect size, as well as prepared and exhilarated to lead this new math mastery initiative IM^3. I broke down all the criteria of Robinson and Hattie's Instructional Leadership qualities listed on (page 13) and reflected on my own practice. This provided me the credibility to lead the conversations when educators and I were discussing best practices. The instructional leadership qualities of Robinson and Hattie helped to shape and provide insight into the direction I wanted to lead the school. The goal was to empower my staff to buy into *"Every student at our school will show growth of more than one year in one school year's time in mathematics."* For example, if a student in 4th grade scored at a level of 3.7 on a summative fall math assessment, I expected that student to grow academically to a level greater than 4.7 on the next assessment. The metric of 3.7 equates to a typical student who is in third grade and the 7th month of school. This is a metric that is used to show student growth and achievement. The metric was created by National Educational Statistics companies and vetted through data linking between state assessments and quarterly assessment. We expected all of our students to achieve more than the 1.0, and as educators, we focused interventions around ensuring these metrics were accomplished. The data is compared from the beginning of the year to the end of the year. Any score that did not improve more than one year in one year's time was a failure to the mission. I wanted to be specific with staff but not authoritarian; such as, all students will practice geometry for 30 minutes a day and use this strategy. Teaching has an art form to it, as well as lesson delivery. It is imperative that you allow the practitioners to customize math instruction for their teaching style to ensure teacher clarity exists.

I was ready to lead and support the educators with the resources and leadership they needed to get the results our community and students desperately deserved.

Summary of Challenging the Status Quo

Knowing your leadership strengths is an integral part of leading an organization, especially when you are leading a change initiative. I find that it is essential to understand what your skills are as a leader so you can address deficiencies and also lead from your strengths. I read the book *Strengths Finder 2.0,* created by Don Clifton and afterward, completed the strengths finder assessment which was very exact and beneficial. The assessment confirmed my strengths as an Achiever, Activator and Restorative leader, which further solidified the path I was planning to follow.

As Simon Sinek states *"People don't buy what you do they buy why you do it."* Vivian Robinson, a New Zealand researcher of principals' effect size, states: "Therefore, the principal's new role is to lead teachers in the process of learning to improve teaching practices while learning alongside them about what works and what does not."

An example of WHAT we do is below:

As I presented a sample rigorous math problem at our monthly professional learning meeting, I impressed upon the educators that I wanted to see more depth-focused math problems. This is the exact type of problem shown below that we used in creating our instructional model IM[3] of high-level math mastery opportunities. More sample problems will be provided in forthcoming chapters and at the end of the book.

Question: There were 14 pizzas for a team party. 10 3/8 were eaten by players. Parents ate 1 ½ of the pizzas. The rest of the pizzas were taken home. How much pizza was eaten at the party? How much was taken home? Use models, numbers or words to explain the rationale for solving.

Chapter Two

The New Vision

"When the vision is clear, the results will appear. Keep your mindset positive as you work your plan, flourish, and always remember why you started."

The Definition of Mastery Learning according to *Open Source*:

Mastery learning (or, as it was initially called, "learning for mastery") is an instructional strategy and educational philosophy, first formally proposed by Benjamin Bloom *in 1968. Mastery learning maintains that students must achieve a level of mastery (e.g., 90% on a knowledge test) in prerequisite knowledge before moving forward to learn subsequent information. If a student does not achieve mastery on the test, they are given additional support in learning and reviewing the information and then tested again. This cycle continues until the learner accomplishes mastery, and they may then move on to the next stage.*

Mastery learning methods suggest that the focus of instruction should be the time required for different students to learn the same material and achieve the same level of mastery. This is very much in contrast with classic models of teaching, which focus more on differences in students' ability and where all students are given approximately the same amount of time to learn and the same set of instructions.

In mastery learning, there is a shift in responsibilities, so that student's failure is more due to the instruction and not necessarily lack of ability on his or her part. Therefore, in a mastery learning environment, the challenge becomes providing enough time and employing instructional strategies so that all students can achieve the same level of learning.

So why does Mastery Level Learning matter in schools? This book will show evidence of how you can increase student learning and accelerate student growth in mathematics using this Mastery-Based learning model IM³. Mastery also allows each learner opportunities to excel in mathematics, regardless of their starting point. When I was in college completing my student teaching course for education, we were never instructed by the professor on what to do with the outlier students in our classroom. Typically, educators tend to teach to "the middle". This grouping of student does not equate to our mission of every student showing more than one year's growth in one year's time. The outliers included the highly advanced child or the child who struggled with mathematics. In the forthcoming chapters, we will give examples of evidence-based practices coupled with educational research to show how you can assist all students in your classroom using this instructional model of mastery in mathematics, IM³.

We will share the evidence of our success!

After months of extensive research, planning and preparation, I was now looking for ways to describe Mastery Learning to my staff. Mastery Learning is similar to personalized learning and other successful frameworks that are part of mainstream education. My entire staff, including myself, was previously trained on differentiation and understood the benefits to personalized learning. The training on differentiation was very robust, however, the majority of the classrooms were still being instructed whole group. As I was preparing to approach my highly effective teachers to implement this new math mastery-learning framework IM³, I wanted to provide them with a glimpse into where this fits comparatively to other frameworks or models. It also allowed me to see which educators I felt could handle a paradigm shift without overworking themselves into burnout.

In the forthcoming paragraphs, I will provide a breakdown of the definitions of: *Personalized Learning, Individualization of Learning* and *Differentiation*. So often in schools, these words and ideas are used interchangeably.

There have been numerous publications on personalized learning and I agree 100% that it is an integral part of Mastery-Based instruction. **Where we see opportunities with Mastery-Based instruction is the fact that mastery of a concept looks different for each child in each class throughout a school.**

Personalized Learning:

Four attributes: voice, co-creation, social construction, self-discovery.
1. Instructor must select assignment
2. Pursue aspirations, investigate problems
3. Learning can happen anytime/anyplace
4. Students have a voice in the content

Individualization (more blended)

-Students are assigned the learning task.
-Students control the pace of mastery. It is personalized in the way technology is used to reflect the needs of the learner.

Differentiation:

Teachers start where the students are to create a range of learning experiences. Students can be assigned or selected themselves.
-- Student choice is within the configuration of what the teacher selects.
--Teacher is still in control of design and management.

Modality	Student Role	Teacher Role	Examples
Personalization	Looks for authentic problems to investigate, uses four attributes	Questions Conferences Feedback	Mastery on Performance
Individualization	Controls the pace and when to demonstrate mastery	Teacher-created tasks	Khan Academy Dreambox Pearson Sm10

| Differentiation | Selects from a range of content or products | Tailors instruction based on needs | Daily 5 choice board, literature circle, varying levels of text on the same topic |

Mastery Learning Paradigm

Here are the mastery concepts and criteria we felt were most important for our students at the K-8 grade level:

1. Students must be able to learn at their own pace.
2. Time is never something that is fixed when learning (students can choose to re-learn a topic or come back to a topic they struggled on).
3. Formative assessments are weighed more than summative assessments.
4. Students can test out of classroom whole group instruction if they pass a mastery quiz on the standard that is being instructed.
5. Students lead the learning and the teachers are the coaches.
6. Learning looks different for each child and they self-differentiate by learning how to use metacognition and also ask for help when they don't reach mastery.
7. The students know where they are going and why they need the information.
8. The summative product of a mastery unit does not have to be a test. It can be a project, video, anchor chart or instructional video emulating the student's depth of knowledge on the topic.

As an instructional leader, it is my full-time commitment to ensure every student reaches mastery in all content areas. The content focus of this book is on Mastery-Based learning in mathematics using this successful instructional model, IM³. Our next book will focus on Mastery-Based learning with students with disabilities. Again, Mastery-Based learning's focus includes students showing more than one year's growth in one year's time. We should continuously be re-evaluating what teaching and assessment practices we use and what strategies yield the greatest results.

Effect Size

As you will read in Chapter **Eight**, our school had plateaued with minimal levels of growth, not enough to make a significant dent in the goal to reach the state benchmarks. Although, as I have learned from Professor John Hattie's research, the majority of everything we do in the classroom leads to growth. **It is the strategies and focus of what the student's do that determines how much growth they will achieve.** When Hattie discusses strategies or compares them, he calculates what is called effect size. Effect size is a comparison between two variables. The variables can be something as simple as a pre/posttest or calculating how many kids knew their math facts prior to implementing a new strategy for fluency.

Hattie's Impact on Educators

We know through Professor Hattie's Meta-Analysis studies that Mastery-Based Learning yields an effect size of .57 years of growth. The average student in the average classroom can grow at approximately a .40 effect size per year with average instruction. When you add the practice of mastery instruction from a highly effective educator, along with other evidence-based instructional strategies, you increase student achievement remarkably.

Educating the teachers on the effect sizes of instructional strategies was very important and imperative to our building goal of more than one year's growth in one year's time. I wanted to create an environment where all educators felt confident trying these evidence-based strategies. I calculated effect sizes from our own educators and compared the results to Hattie's evidence-based analysis. This data allowed all interested and vested math mastery educators using this instructional model IM^3 to see how these strategies have worked and the teachers "reward" of higher student achievement outweighed the risks of trying a new strategy.

The Ship Bound for Master Island

As previously mentioned in chapter one, my goal was to encourage the staff to "board the ship to Mastery Island". It was imperative as a leader, to understand the strengths of my staff. I used data from classroom walkthroughs, as well as summative data from state assessments to formulate my evaluations. In addition, I collated and presented data on student growth on quarterly and formative assessments to ensure I was selecting the correct educators to lead this initiative. I believe all educators have opportunities to improve and wanted to focus on the educators who had the readiness and desire to exceed exponentially. I will use the analogy of Navigators, Aspiring Navigators, Riders and Anchors as the depiction for the groups of educators.

Navigators: These are the educators who are striving to be the best. Navigators are **All-Star** educators who are hungry to be challenged and see this mastery initiative as a way to empower all learners, as well as themselves. Most schools have about 20% of their staff fit this description. They tend to stay in their rooms and only associate with other Navigators. They are less apt to show the successes or share the strategies they use unless they are asked. This group comprises a small percentage of the school but can be very powerful in collaborative groups, sometimes referred to as PLC's (Professional Learning Communities). I selected a small sample size of one Navigator to start this Mastery-Based initiative. My full intention was for this initiative to be successful. I started in small steps and wanted to grow this initiative organically, once we had finite data to provide to other Navigators and Aspiring Navigators. As the Navigator and I are engaging in this endeavor, I made it apparent that I have set aside specific times to assist with implementation, remediation and interventions. I made it clear that this was not a teacher initiative but a journey we were going to partake in together to ensure it was scalable and had the data to prove the success. Some of the traits of Navigators are:

1. They have strong self-monitoring skills.
2. Navigators perceive large and meaningful patterns.
3. Navigators spend relatively more time analyzing problems carefully and quantitatively.
4. Navigators represent problems at a deep level and can analyze and anticipate errors of students.

As a Lead Learner in an organization, these are qualities that should also be a part of your skill set!

Now meet the Navigator who was selected

Abbey Mezinko is the teacher Navigator and co-author of this book. She will provide you with specific examples and descriptions of how to implement this instructional model of mastery-based learning, IM^3, in your classroom. I have witnessed Abbey attending extensive training through professional learning and planning the implementation of Hattie's evidence-based strategies during classroom planning and instruction. She also uses differentiation on a tireless basis. When I conducted walkthroughs in Abbey's class, I observed the use of student-created anchor charts, Jigsaw's, as well as, complete and total student engagement on instruction. I also viewed her flipping the "I Do, We Do, You Do" framework. By changing and doing the "we do" first it created a culture of inquiry and perseverance. She did not use this model all the time, however, when she did use the inverted model it created excitement and led to increased student inquiry. She also incorporated the Daily 3 math centers in her classroom and having predetermined time working with specific students in small groups. In support of Abbey and this new initiative, we meet regularly and discuss student achievement and growth. We converse daily about specific students' growth and achievement, and other factors that may provide insight into how I can support her and the students in this important instructional model of mastery-based model of mathematics IM³.

Inside the Navigator's Classroom

<u>Vignette inside Co-Author Abbey Mezinko's 3rd Grade classroom:</u>

One of the many lessons I observed from this dynamic educator was on Number Sense. As she was explaining the strategies to her learners she made it known that knowing one strategy was a basic level of mastery but to truly master the content you needed to understand all of the following instructional strategies. Students who had mastery in Number Sense should be able to use the following strategies when solving problems.

1. Mental math
2. Estimation
3. Numerical Equivalents
4. Use of Benchmarks, like ½ is 50%
5. A sense of order and Number Magnitude
6. Place Value as needed for understanding; why 536 is 500 + 30 + 6

Problem: *Given a problem with 1654, 4923, and 587 you can ask:*

Which is the greatest and which is the least?
About how much is the sum?
How did you get that answer?
Which number is different from the other two? In what ways?
These questions allowed her to gauge in a formative way, how her students understood the math concept of number sense.
She also uses the question strands below when asking number sense questions in her classroom:

1. Which is the most or greatest? How do you know?
2. Which is the least or smallest? How do you know?
3. What else can you tell me about the above numbers?
4. How else can we express the numbers? Is there still another way?
5. About how much would that be? How did you get that?

After viewing this lesson and seeing the multiple strategies she was using to provide learning to all students, I knew that she had the ability to differentiate, create tasks that were rich in math content, and also had a thorough understanding of math standards and success criteria for her students. This was a typical lesson, not one that was created for an evaluation.

Aspiring Navigators: This is where about 50% of your staff resides and has the potential to become Navigators with the right coaching from administrators and the collaborative efficacy of the PLC's and team members. They are quick to want to try new initiatives but need the scaffolds put in place by the administration to ensure they are successful. The Aspiring Navigators can give you massive amounts of growth, especially when working collaboratively with the Navigators.

When I speak with students about what they learn in their classrooms, the students in Aspiring Navigators classrooms always love their educator and find him/her very engaged with what they are learning. One of the differences between the Navigators and Aspiring Navigators is experience-implementing new school initiatives and understanding which strategy works best for which student in what content area. This is something that is a learnable skill. Some of the key characteristics that Aspiring Navigators have are that they are willing to try and implement evidence-based strategies but struggle with full implementation. Once they are shown through practice, they become more confident. Matching them with a Navigator will accelerate their productivity and also improve their confidence and reinforce their enthusiasm.

Some of the traits of Aspiring Navigators are:
1. Try to implement too many new strategies without ensuring the students fully understand the process.
2. Willing to try any new strategy and implement with fidelity.
3. Usually the 1st to volunteer for committees or anything that benefits students.
4. Self-reflective and sometimes unable to see the positive impact they are having on student achievement.
5. Eager to attend professional learning and very engaged when any new learning opportunity presents itself.

6. Over reliant on "new" initiatives and sometimes looses trust in their previously successful practices. Hence, "New is not always better".
7. They will also sometimes over analyze the amount of time needed to implement initiatives.

" No matter how many mistakes you make or how slow you progress, you are still way ahead of everyone who isn't trying."
Tony Robbins

Riders: About 20% of my staff resides in this paradigm. These are the educators who are along for the ride. They do not standout, they are just happy seeing compliant students completing worksheets. As we know from Hattie's research, students who come to school, regardless of their instructor, learn things. Hattie has evidence that students can grow .2 to .4 years during a school year even in ineffective classrooms. He further states with just average instruction, the students can gain .32. That is still below the average growth norm of .4. The caveat is that unless an instructional strategy shows an effect size of .4 or higher, there is more likely a better practice available.

Some of the traits you will notice with the Riders are:
1. Low personalization of learning, mostly whole group.
2. They overestimate how much their students are learning in their class and lack the ability to properly use formative assessments and formative data.
3. They use procedures to ensure the classroom is quiet and the students appear to be in a "boredom trance".

4. They will attend professional development more as a means to escape "school". Lack of implementation after professional learning.
5. Will normally wait till the very last day to accomplish any task and appear overwhelmed or unsure.

Anchors: This will comprise about 10% of your staff, and they stay employed for social reasons. They will combat or find an issue in everything you do. If you ask for opinions, they won't acknowledge or respond. They will do everything in their power to pull the Riders down to their paradigm. They are experts in manipulation and turning positive into negative in schools. Don't underestimate the power these Anchors have in your organization. My opinion is to document what these educators do in the classroom and follow your districts protocols for termination. These educators are usually the teachers who yell at kids and blame them for not showing growth. My recommendation is to follow a process such as this:

1. Conference with the Anchors and explain the areas that need to improve. Make sure you have data to support your statements.
2. Offer support, such as visiting other teachers' classrooms, professional learning, modeling of lessons, etc.
3. If not successful, place on an improvement plan and assign two goals from the standards of educators that are related to the deficiency of the teacher. Support and document everything you are doing to assist the Anchor in improving.
4. If growth is not being shown, contact your human resource department and recommend they assist. This is not a pleasant experience and one that few leaders are willing to take but is necessary if you want to improve your school.

Some of the traits you will notice with Anchors are:
1. They will have an unwavering focus on anything non-academic. They will assist with anything non-academic, lead potlucks, for example.
2. Very little movement around the classroom with an abundance of worksheets is the means of instruction.
3. After a new initiative is implemented, the first to say, "Another new initiative that won't work."
4. Are the last to arrive and the first to leave when school is over. Celebrating the end of everyday as they leave exhausted and the students leave refreshed.
5. They are known as the strong disciplinarians as the students are not allowed to move freely in the class. The educator stresses compliance far more over student engagement.

When we look at rigor in Navigators and Aspiring Navigators classrooms, we see more problems at the Mastery Level of 2 or 3.

Mastery Level 1: Recall, solving algorithmically, substituting numbers in a formula, one-step word problems. RTI would fall under Mastery Level 1.

Mastery Level 2: Multi-step word problems, apply more than one strategy to solve a problem, rely on background knowledge from previous grades to solve the problem. The majority of state assessment questions fall under this level.

Mastery Level 3: Solve multi-step word problems and justify the result. There is evidence of multiple standards and multiple mathematical practices in the question and result.

Here are a few sample problems. Decide which Level of Mastery (Level 1, Level 2 or Level 3) these questions could apply to and why? The answers are also in the back of the book.

<u>**Question #A   6th grade fraction problem**</u>:
John gave half of his stamps to Jim. Jim gave half of his stamps to Carla. Carla gave 1/4 of the stamps given to her to Thomas and kept the remaining 12. How many stamps did John start with?

Mastery Level 1
Mastery Level 2
Mastery Level 3
Your Choice:

Question #B   **4th grade fraction problem:**

1. What fraction might be slightly larger and slightly smaller than $\frac{1}{3}$?

2. Ask students to select three fractions that they could easily compare to 4/6 and explain why the comparisons are easy for them. This will help gauge student understanding.

3. Ask why 3/10 is not greater than $\frac{1}{2}$ even though 3>1 and 10>2.

Mastery Level 1
Mastery Level 2
Mastery Level 3
Your Choice:

Questions #C   **2nd grade fraction problem:**

 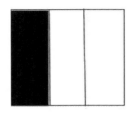 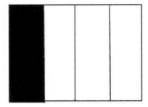

1st rectangle was presented to students. They were asked why it is possible for the exact same rectangle (1st one) to be half of one rectangle, yet one third or one fourth of another. These are very simple, yet powerful differences

Mastery Level 1
Mastery Level 2
Mastery Level 3
Your Choice:

Question #D   5th grade fraction problem:

The table below shows the length of ribbon, in yards, needed to make different art projects.

Project	Length of Ribbon (in yards)
Flower	$1\frac{3}{4}$
Bulletin board	$3\frac{1}{3}$
Costume	2
Mask	$\frac{1}{3}$
Puppet	$2\frac{1}{2}$
Picture frame	$\frac{1}{4}$

Lance has $3\frac{2}{3}$ yards of ribbon. He is making a puppet. How much ribbon, in yards, will Lance have left?

☐ Yards

Mastery Level 1

Mastery Level 2

Mastery Level 3

Your Choice:

Question # E   **5th-6th grade problem:**

Here is a sample problem which in terms of Rigor is viewed as a surface level question. However, the questioning the educator uses makes the problem far more rigorous and utilizes the skill of Planning and Prediction (Effect Size .76). It is also a problem that supports cooperative learning (Effect size .40).

George's Pizza Shop

Small Pizza   **Medium Pizza**

6 inches in diameter   9 inches in diameter

6 slices   8 slices

$ 5.75 $ 8.95

Questions:

1. Which pizza is the better buy?
2. How much cheaper is one slice of the small pizza?
3. How much bigger or smaller is one slice of the medium pizza than one slice of the small pizza?
4. I need to feed 20 people and each person should get about 25 square inches of pizza. Which pizzas should I buy, how many, and what will it cost?
5. Design and describe a large pizza, including the diameter, the number of slices, and its cost. Explain how you made your choices.

Mastery Level 1   Mastery Level 2   Mastery Level 3

Question #F   5th-6th grade problem

2 ¼ was written on the board in the class.

The teacher simply asked the students to work with their elbow partner and to come up with at least three things they see on the board as it relates to 2 ¼.

The ideas are written on the board such as:

Mixed Number

Whole Number

Fraction

I see 2.25

I see 9/4

Once some of the above have been notated, the following questions were asked in no apparent order:

1. What makes 2 ¼ a mixed number?
2. Why is 2.25 equivalent to 2 ¼?
3. Can you name another decimal equivalent?
4. What do we call 9/4?
5. Why is 9/4 equivalent to 2 ¼?
6. Which number is the numerator and denominator?

These questions allow all levels of learners to engage in math and also provides some deeper level of discussion for groups.

Mastery Level 1

Mastery Level 2

Mastery Level 3

What does a Mastery Educator "look like"?

"The time is always right, to do what's right."
Martin Luther King Jr.

Educators who are ready for Mastery Implementation are observed:
1. Having positive relationships with learners, they use formative checks more frequently than summative assessments.
2. Giving feedback.
3. Engaging in dialogue with students.
4. Providing challenging questions every day.
5. Managing classroom, so learning is the critical focus for students, not behavior.

The above five evidence-based practices are not an all-inclusive list. However, the effect size of the five items listed, when done correctly, will assist the classroom educator with reaching the school's goal of more than one year's growth in one year's time.

To further move our educators toward this IM^3 instructional model, I provide on a biweekly basis, video vignettes of master teachers using successful practices. In addition to videos, I am constantly taking and recording effective lessons from within our building and sharing them in a blog format with all stakeholders. Through daily learning walkthroughs, I will send a quick email with comments providing coaching and positive reinforcement to the educators. As the Lead Learner, it is imperative that your coaching style is viewed as positive. It is also important to assist educators by looking for other professional learning opportunities through the various resources available today. By having open, data-oriented conversations, you can communicate with staff and find out how you can assist them with their professional learning goals.

Educators who are ready for Mastery implementation never do the following:
1. Use grading as a punishment.
2. Conflict behavior with grades.
3. Elevate quiet compliance over academic work.
4. Use worksheets excessively.
5. Accept low quality work as a student's personal best.
6. Evaluate their impact by the amount of curriculum they cover.

When I am conducting learning walks and see one of the above six items being practiced by an educator, I will engage them at some point throughout the day and ask a question such as "What evidence do you have that worksheets actively engage students and show academic growth toward our school's goal of showing more than one year's growth in one year's time?"

Growth and Effect Size

As I stated in Chapter One, before our mastery initiative began, we did increase the standardized test scores of the majority of our students who were rated Limited to a rate of Basic or above based on a scale of: Limited, Basic, Proficient, Accelerated, and Advanced. We were not pleased with this growth, as students were still more than one grade level behind where they should have been at this point. Yes, some students were showing a year's growth, but barely. We knew we had to find other strategies or methodologies to gain more than a year's growth to have any chance of meeting our goal of more than one year's growth in one year's time. From the outside, it looks like we are showing growth and according to the state, we are showing high levels of growth. When we analyzed all the data as stated before, we knew that if we used more effective practices, we could show increased gains in classrooms with Navigators, Aspiring Navigators and Riders.

Here are some suggestions when conducting learning walks in classrooms. Assisting educators with growth is an ongoing process and one in which, as a leader, a high portion of your time should be devoted to.

1. Ensure that the sample size is as large as possible. The smaller the sample, the more variance there is in the numbers and the impact it creates. This implies that doing multiple learning walks and witnessing consistent practices ensures that it is a standard practice and not just an anomaly.
2. As a leader, do not use effect size data or any data piece as a "stick." The data should be a catalyst for conversation not for evaluation. Allow the teachers to view the data and dissect it. Your role should be to ask questions.
3. One easy way, as a leader, to provide some simple feedback is by collecting participation and movement data for the educator during direct instruction. This information may open up a conversation on seating, group work, the educator's movement, partiality to a student, or part of a room. Ask the educator for a copy of their seating chart and just track lines where they move in the room and tally how many times a specific student is called on to answer a question.
4. Another simple and effective administrative way to support mastery based teaching is to tabulate how many questions the

students ask during an observed lesson. You will find that very few questions are related to the content, rather most are procedural. This data will allow educators to reflect and plan on incorporating more student opportunities for inquiry type questions and responses.
5. One of the most important coaching strategies is to have academic conversations with educators, as well as having this type of conversation in PLC's with multiple educators. This can include peer-to-peer observation with academic conversations to follow. This practice has shown to increase self-efficacy and also improve culture and climate in the building.

Making Crucial Conversations Safe

Here are some common themes that should take place during conversations with employees:

1. Make it safe to converse about the school topic: "When purpose is at risk, the conversation will evolve into a debate."

2. Awareness: Are you noticing or ignoring the safety level of the participants in the dialogue; such as realizing the tone of the person you are conversing with becoming elevated or labored. Once the safety level has been breached, the conversation turns into a debate. This is imperative for the speaker to understand and redirect the conversation when they notice this starting to occur. Once it happens, it will be extremely difficult to garner support.

3. Observation: Are you watering down the conversation to make it safe? (This strategy avoids the real problem)

4. No pretending, sugarcoating or faking.

Summary of the New Vision

"The only thing worse than being blind is having sight but no vision"
Hellen Keller

Mastery is a hybrid of Personalization of Learning, Differentiation and Individualization. By combining the components of each, we were able to create an instructional model IM³ that has proven highly effective based upon the results of the most current state summative math assessments. Understanding which educators are the Navigators, Aspiring Navigators, Riders and Anchors is imperative as you look to build capacity within your staff. As an Instructional Leader, the majority of your time should be spent coaching the educators who are poised to implement this initiative.

In summary, I hope that you can use this paradigm of staff alignment with your current staff and begin to build your capacity to coach and ensuring that all students can reach more than one year's growth in one year's time.

Using the problems on pages 32-37 will provide a learning opportunity for you and your staff at an upcoming staff meeting. I am suggesting you share these math questions with your staff and request them to solve them in table groups. After reading and becoming familiar with the IM³ model of instruction have your staff decide which level the problems on page 32-37 reflect. Are they Mastery Level1, Mastery Level 2 or Mastery Level 3?

Chapter Three

Instructional Leadership and Math Mastery IM³

"The reality is that the only way change comes is when you lead by example."

Anne Wojcicki

During the math mastery-based pre-planning phase, I studied best practices on improving student attendance, reducing classroom interruptions, and how to create a continues, positive school culture and climate. I spent the first few months in the summer, before implementation, ensuring the above-mentioned items had my full attention. Abbey (Co-Author), who was selected to lead the initiative as our schools first mastery-based teacher, was working on an implementation plan, as well. We were co-planning so that this new Math Mastery-Based Initiative and this instructional model, IM³ would be a success. I continued to readjust, foresee and correct problems before they could become future problems. I will provide examples of teacher and student efficacy, improving attendance, behavior management, parent buy-in, intervention team and numerous sample problems of successful math strategies.

  One of my first steps in creating a positive learning environment for students and improving student attendance was to make sure students had everything they needed to feel successful. I solicited donations from local businesses for clothing and hygiene items. Our current school nurse also helps to ensure students have essential items they may need. Students who lack school attire are provided with it from the school office, so they do not miss instructional time. We do have a basic uniform policy, as a district, which creates some additional burdens on families. Therefore, it was crucial that our school counselor, nurse, and all other stakeholders were on board with ensuring we had the necessary resources and empathy to assist students. We needed everyone to quickly diagnose an issue or find a resource to allow our learners to come to school or return to class as soon as possible. For instance, we noticed students who struggled with academic content wanted to see the nurse at times when the learning in their classroom became too difficult for them. We did not prevent students from going to the nurse in the beginning. However, the nurse spent time speaking with the kids and confirming their thoughts of anxiety or fear of failure. Once we were aware of these student issues, we could build supports in the classroom.

Teacher and Student Self-Efficacy

One of the first cultural norms we faced with this new Mastery-Based initiative was the students were identified far below their grade level norm. While yes, we agree, Socioeconomic Status does have a high negative effect size (.52), we knew that if we chose to focus on teacher and student efficacy instead, we could mitigate the adverse effect size and show growth. SERC Carleton College describes student efficacy as *Students' successful experiences boost self-efficacy, while failures erode it. This is the most robust source of self-efficacy. Vicarious experience - Observing a peer succeed at a task can strengthen beliefs in one's own abilities.* The above definition highlights the exact effect we were hoping to stimulate in our school culture by improving students' beliefs in their skills, as well as developing teacher efficacy. Self-efficacy is gaining a lot of traction in educational communities with varying definitions. Self-efficacy for my current staff and myself can be summarized as ...*the belief each child has the ability to reach the mastery level of the task they are completing*. We have found that when students start trying Mastery-Based lessons and assessments, they lack perseverance. We spend time daily, via morning announcements, reviewing the Habits of the Mind on perseverance. The Habits of the Mind are a group of 16 soft skills that were created by Arthur Costa and his associates. The skills provide student-friendly definitions and all pertain to skills that 21st century learners and specifically, mastery-level learners, need to be successful.

One of the evidence-based practices that educators and students can use that will improve the skill of perseverance is the *Strategy of Error Analysis*. The Error Analysis Strategy is broken down as:

Step 1: Have students analyze their most recent chapter test or assessment
Step 2: Go over the correct answers with the students
Step 3: Have students make corrections on their tests
Step 4: Have them find a section in their math notebook and label it "Error Growth." Ensure that these procedures are modeled and discussed prior to implementation.
Step 5: Create 3 columns as such:

The Situation	Violation	Correction
3 - (7-5)	Did not Distribute the negative sign	3-7+5=1
3-7-5=9		
Given Points (3,4) (6,7)	Did not use the formula correctly. Y_2 in (x_2, y_2) should be on top.	
Find the Slope		
6-3 / 7-4		M=7-4/6-3 =1
Add 2/7 + 3/8 = 5/15	Did not find the common denominator	16/56 +21/56 =37/56

This strategy assists with metacognition, as well as helping kids understand what their strengths are and where they need to spend more time improving. We have found that when students have Mastery experiences, it boosts their self-efficacy.

Teacher Efficacy

I spent time deciphering teacher efficacy. As a leader, I wanted to be more aware of how I could support and maximize educators' perceptions of themselves. I focused on a few critical items that made implementation of the Math Mastery Initiative IM ^{3} more manageable and successful. Examples of the support I provided for improvement in teacher-efficacy are:

1. Calculating the effect size of student growth on math formative assessments. Educators provided pre/post test data to me so I could assist them with analyzing the data. These staff members were mainly my Navigators and Aspiring Navigators who were seeking my assistance to help them evaluate their effectiveness.
2. Model how educators can use the math formative and summative data to stimulate student growth. Share evidence-based research to show that the strategies they are using in this Math Mastery-Based Initiative IM^3 are working.
3. Provide classroom behavioral support when implementing the above initiative. Teachers are "stepping outside of the box" and may need support. Your educators need to feel secure and safe and trust that you will keep the items that drain their energy away from their implementation of this new initiative.
4. Ensure parents understand that you support this new Math Mastery-Based Initiative IM^3 and why it will benefit their child or children. We invite our parents to take part in this Mastery process through parent meetings, newsletters and announcements. Anytime we are making decisions that will affect their child or children, we always include our parents.

Lead Learner Leads Intervention Time

"You will never reach your destination if you stop and throw stones at every dog that barks." Winston Churchill

As I was planning the school year for this new initiative, I felt as the instructional leader, I should implement an intervention time where I work with students. I use a 30-minute block of time each day to work with a selected group of learners on math interventions. I select, via formative data, some of our lowest performing students in math and work with them on areas where they struggle. This intervention time allows our classroom educators to focus on other small groups of students, which maximizes the instruction in the classroom. Assisting lower performing students also allows the students to see that I am vested in their education. This is a positive for our school culture, and it reduces the number of behavior infractions, as I am building a relationship with all students.

Some suggestions for interventions are:
1. Utilize free online math programs.
2. Have students work on Self-Organized Learning Prompts. SOLE was created by Professor Sugatra Mitra from India. It is the personalization of questions for each child. There is a resource site that gives you great math questions to ask students. If you search for SOLE, you will find numerous resources. I have the kids complete at least two SOLE questions per week, as it helps with collaboration and writing in mathematics.
3. Have peer-to-peer tutoring in the intervention time. It is a great way to enhance school culture by having an older student instruct a younger student on the area where they are struggling.

4. Have educators in your building record, via media, their instruction on specific standards. For instance, if an 8th grade student is struggling with the Pythagorean Theorem after his/her classroom teacher has instructed the class, he/she can go to the shared drive and watch another teacher, via recorded video, instruct a lesson on the Pythagorean Theorem. We have found this to be an integral part of our intervention process to create a culture of learning.

As we are in a "tested" world, where students are required to take tests, it is essential to understand which students need specific resources. The educators should have daily formative checks and work samples available to use for this intervention time. Having the Lead Learner lead this intervention initiative helps to bridge the gap between administration and educators and ensures that the principal's office and skill set is deemed as an extension of the classroom.

Improving Attendance

We, in the education arena, all want to improve student attendance. All districts and states base school successes partially on student attendance. As a principal, I knew if I wanted the Math Mastery Initiative IM^3 to work and all students to grow more than one year's growth in one year's time, this had to be at the forefront of my agenda. I specifically target learners who are struggling with school attendance and build a relationship with them. I encourage the students to greet me in the hallway each morning as they arrive for school so I can acknowledge their attendance. As John Maxwell stated numerous times *"People don't care how much you know until they know how much you care."* Simply acknowledging student attendance and celebrating classroom perfect attendance on the morning announcements further encourages students to attend school. We also make a point to seek out the children who have significantly improved their attendance and have a celebration with them. This attendance process is ongoing each day and is paramount to the success of any initiative but specifically to this new Math Mastery Initiative IM³.

I also have students, who have shown attendance improvement, join me for lunch on certain days so I can continue to establish and maintain a positive relationship with them. In essence, I leverage my relationships with students to enable them to feel confident and provide an outlet for them to express any frustration they may have toward school or the school setting. As I began to establish relationships with the low attendance learners, they began to confide in me about specific academic struggles they have. I learned from them which teachers they struggled with and which content they felt was too hard. This information was paramount as I looked for ways to continue to improve their attendance and their academics.

Behavior Management

Behavior management is one of the most critical structures you can provide for your staff. A one-size fits all behavior framework will not work for all students and all schools. While leading the school for the past few years, I have reviewed various models and frameworks and vetted the most successful for us. I have found that Love and Logic, PBIS and Restorative Justice behavior frameworks work the best for my current school. As I began to understand each program and their specifics, it occurred to me that we needed pieces of each to fit the structures of our school. These are all vetted programs that will give your staff and school the structure that is needed to pursue a school culture that is ready for the Math Mastery Initiative IM³. As you are working on the behavioral management piece of implementing mastery, it is essential to also revisit school safety and the emotional safety of the learners. I find it necessary to practice fire, tornado, and ALICE drills more than the required amount. I want to ensure my staff and learners can focus on instruction and understand they are prepared in the unlikely event of an emergency.

Another critical component for you as a lead learner is to ensure instruction is taking place when students are in your office for disciplinary reasons. The office provides a great location and venue for a quick intervention. I begin by establishing a relationship prior to issuing a consequence. It is imperative to investigate to see if the poor behavior choices were a result of academic struggle or something else. As I work with principals and educators, I insist that principals keep a plethora of books available for student selection when they are in your office. While you are reviewing any behavior infractions, it is vital that instruction is still taking place. Having students read is a simple way for them to gain more reading time while also showing them you value them as a learner. It is vital that you focus on the most important role you have, which is as an instructional leader. The students in the school should see the office of the instructional leader as another classroom. It is imperative that the students see every adult in the school as an advocate for their success. For a leader to indeed drive instruction, he or she must be focused on student achievement.

Behavior management and excellent student attendance are two very important daily focuses for school success. Using the morning announcements or other forms of media to share building successes is a powerful tool to increase student attendance and improve student behavior. Having visual representations of the goals of the school on the walls are visible reminders to all students that their attendance and behavior matters. For instance, place a chart with the school's goals for attendance and behavior referrals in a visible common area. Update these charts daily or at least weekly showing the current data and have conversations with students on how they impact the results.

These are some of the current practices that I employ daily in my building:

1. Greet all students as they enter the building in the morning with either a fist bump or high five.
2. During daily classroom walkthroughs, have academic conversations with students showing you are vested in the educational process.
3. When you notice infractions taking place, be clear that this is not an acceptable action from a learner at your school.
4. When you notice a student do a random act of kindness, praise the student and encourage more acts of kindness
5. Model expectations for learners by cleaning up paper towels or garbage on the floor and subsequently praise when I notice a student emulating my action.
6. Give shouts to staff members when you notice them doing something exceptional.
7. Create a positive referral system for students so teachers can nominate a student when they notice they do something that is exceptional and not part of the norm.

All of the above practices will enhance a positive school environment and allow any initiative that is chosen to be completed successfully.

"For a child to learn something new, it needs to be repeated an average of 8 times. For the same child to unlearn an old behavior and replace with a new behavior, the new behavior must be repeated an average of 28 times." Harry Wong

Parent Buy-In

We have fantastic parents at our school. Even though our attendance at parent-teacher conferences is not 100%, we believe our parents do the very best they can. About 35% of our parents have graduated high school, and 7% attended college. We see this as a tremendous opportunity to provide growth options for entire families. We are engrossed in using Mastery to change family structures. "It takes a small rock thrown into a lake to make large ripples that continue." Our mission is to help move a person in each family toward college and career readiness. We believe that mastery is the positive process.

As with any new initiative, it is important to have as many stakeholders involved in the process. Parents are key stakeholders in the mastery development and we encourage them to join in the educational process through Mastery Days. At the January PTO meeting, Abbey and five of her students modeled a math mastery based project showing Mastery as our new school initiative. We invited school board members, parents and other stakeholders. We provided a Question and Answer session at the end for parents or stakeholders to ask the students or educator questions on the initiative.

We believe that Mastery is a positive process. We have results that show how it brings parents into the classroom for Mastery awards, for instance. Students are energized to tackle engineering design challenges and the entire required school curriculum. With the educational enthusiasm that our learners embody, we believe Mastery is contagious and will continue to create growth opportunities for the entire family of our students.

Master Schedule

For personalization of learning to occur, the school's master schedule must be designed to allow for intervention time and also time for Professional Learning Community Meetings. One of the responsibilities that administrators have control over is the master schedule. In many situations, schedules are built around lunchtimes and specialists. I create our master schedule around the most productive educators. Educators, who show the most growth, use the most effective evidence-based strategies, and who use Mastery as a means of personalized assessment, need this time together to plan and share ideas. Another critical piece of schedule design is to try and find a way for your educators to have common planning time with their grade level peers. Collaboration amongst peers is a vital piece in implementing Mastery-Based Initiative. Every opportunity should be made to have collaboration available for educators during the school day. The educators must have enough material and time to co-plan with their peers to ensure they have the best possible lessons to maximize instructional time.

<u>Here are some items that I feel are paramount to assist your educators with this new Math Mastery Initiative IM^3:</u>

1. Create the school's master schedule to allow for educators to have time in teacher grade level meetings to work on this Math Mastery Initiative together.
2. Spend extra time and effort to avoid adding more non-instructional items to their job duties. This includes: not asking them to serve on various committees, fundraisers or other activities that steal the time away from this initiative.
3. Minimize office calls to their rooms.

4. Provide information via staff blogs instead of having meetings just to meet and provide un-academic information.
5. Ensure a schoolwide behavior framework is in place and you lead the process of ensuring it is consistent and student-centered.
6. Having Tier 2 and Tier 3 services in place for learners who struggle with behaviors and need additional academic support.
7. Staff meeting time should be maximized for professional learning or collective staff efficacy.

Note: You will find that the Mastery teachers and students working on Mastery do not like to be out of their classrooms. Also, behavior issues are very minimal.

The above items are not a complete list. Imagine being in an in-depth learning state with significant momentum and the phone rings to ask if a student is present today.

Days are for People; Nights are for Paperwork!!!

What strategies can you support as a Lead Learner to assist with Math Mastery?

I found the most impactful approach, as a leader in my building was to collaboratively score student work anonymously. I believe that the days are for students and the nights are for paperwork. Do not try to lead this initiative from your office! Your office can be used at times to work with students completing interventions. However, you should be spending a large part of your day with the practitioners. I have educators who are part of the Mastery Process, who place student sample math work in my mailbox either graded or not, and I will make comments on the papers. I also look to see what strategies the students and educators are using for this content area. The above practices help me track and ensure the educators have enough "tools" in their toolbox. If I notice through collaboration with a staff member that they need additional support with strategies or are willing to grow as a teacher leader, I will find professional learning opportunities to help fill their tool chest.

Some of the interventions that we currently use are:
1. Micro-progressions of content
2. Peer to peer tutoring
3. Adult mentors
4. Computerized programs for math fluency such as Prodigy, Xtra Math, IXL, Reflex Math and various others
5. After-school tutoring

School Math Mastery Days

One of the ways that we bring Math Mastery level learning to light is to have a Math Mastery Day every 9 weeks. Each student who has reached math mastery on a grade level standard will choose one of the mastered topics and make a presentation to the principal and limited guests. As a school, we invite parents and guardians in to witness the progression of their child's educational journey. It assists with parent relationships and further connects the school community to the learning. We have found this to be a fantastic way to celebrate success. It also provides confirmation to the student and feedback to the educator on how well their students engaged the audience and explained the content. The students are the teachers on these Math Mastery Days, and this helps build on other skills such as public speaking and confidence, which leads to a more educationally sound student. This practice of Mastery Days goes on further to bridge the gap between parents and the school.

Intervention Team

"If your presence doesn't add value, your absence won't make a difference."

Most Districts and schools have definitions for what Intervention Teams look like. We have an Intervention Response Team, which addresses children who are being tested for academic deficiencies and who also need additional behavioral support. We believe and trust that as we fully implement this Math Mastery Initiative IM[3], we will no longer have a need for Intervention Response Teams. We will meet students at their academic level and scaffold the rigor in the content area to their current capability. The "true" intervention team at my school consists of four educators comprised of Navigators and Aspiring Navigators who have devoted their life and purpose to individualizing instruction. In any organization, you have support from approximately 80% of the stakeholders. While we have buy-in from the majority, there are some who have yet to see the importance of this instructional model of math mastery work. The Anchors constantly believe their students who are not showing growth are either behaviorally handicapped or should be in special education. The intervention team bears the brunt of these complaints from the Anchors. We require evidence, other than personal opinion, when making any decisions. This includes detailed interventions depicting the problem behavior and skill, as well as pre/post data on the interventions. The Anchors are masterful at providing, on a daily basis, statements such as "My class is so low, I have three or four kids who are definitely special education students." Other comments from Anchors, such as "I have been teaching for a long time, and his behavior is definitely behavioral handicapped" are often said non-chalantly. The Intervention Team's role is to require evidence that the required interventions are performed with fidelity. It is far from a perfect system. The process of having a panel of school staff who represent the teaching body, making decisions on special education services, ensures every student has an advocate. As a team, we will push back the Anchors and ask for intervention data that substantiates their opinion. The majority of the time, Anchors do not want to complete the work needed to move forward. The quiet child who has learning issues flies under the radar in Anchor's classrooms, as they are compliant children. Compliance is what makes Anchors happy and has them continuing to think they are effective educators.

RTI still plays a role in mastery education in our classrooms. There is always a need to remediate skills that were not mastered in previous grades. We use eight lesson intervention cycles with students who are on a particular standard-below mastery. We have tried various RTI programs and have most recently selected Delta Math as our RTI program. If you are unable to purchase Delta Math, it is something that can be created within PLC's. You want to look for the standards of the previous grades to ensure students have the background information to be successful when working with current grade level content. For instance, if we are working on multi-digit subtraction in 3rd grade and the students are struggling with subtraction facts, we will create an intervention group for those learners. We will instruct them on strategies they can use to master that previous standard. Since we only use an 8-day pre/post-test model, we do see some growth but not necessarily complete mastery. Our goal is to instruct the learners on the strategies that can assist them with mastery. We also create a custom tailored, computer-aided program to support the learners during tutoring time or other academic intervention time. As the Instructional Leader, you should spend time to vet and look for new resources or products that may enhance mastery and interventions. There are numerous math products that come to market each year, all promising colossal student math growth. We have tried some products and we agree with Professor Hattie's research that such products have a minimal effect size on student growth.

We incorporate approximately 20-30 minutes each day for interventions. This is not an abundance of time, however, it is enough to mitigate one standard for each child per week using a rotation. As mentioned previously, educators in the building videotape themselves teaching specific standards and sharing them in a shared drive for students to use when needed. As an instructional leader, I also create 1-2 videos per month to add to our collection of instructional videos. This media platform allows learners to select a video to help them when they are struggling with a content area. Our educators are prominent advocates of KHAN Academy, and direct students there when applicable. Students prefer staff & peer math videos, as they can't see the KHAN Academy instructors. Kahn Academy videos just show a whiteboard with a voice explaining the content. The viewer never sees the face or body of who is presenting the material. We have found through our experience in urban environments, the learners like authentic instruction versus webcast types of learning. By having our own educators create specific videos on the math power standards, the kids can relate the content to the instructor. It also shows the end user that the entire school is on board with assisting students with improving their learning. When the students are attempting to learn a specific skill and use a school created video, it personalizes it for the child. We have also uploaded videos to the teaching channel for our learners to view and use. We use google drive and place all the videos in a folder and then share the folder with students to allow them access.

So, the instructional model of mastery in mathematics, IM³, that Abbey will be discussing in the next few chapters will demonstrate how all of the above ideas or programs integrate into a classroom. The real strength of this initiative is the practitioners who make it happen every day in the classroom.

Summary of Instructional Leader Portion of Math Mastery-Based Learning IM³

You will now have the opportunity to read how this exceptional educator, Abbey, implemented this initiative and subsequently had all of her students pass the most recent State exam in mathematics.

When we began to investigate and create the Math Mastery Initiative IM³ we had many doubts that we could implement it in the timeframe of 6 months to 1 year and ensure fidelity. We planned and persevered in creating a system that is scalable and being scaled in our school now. We took detailed notes and data points when calculating the effect sizes of the various educators and evidence-based practices. We wanted to be sure that we were within the norm, comparative to John Hattie's meta-analysis. We were within an acceptable range and also found some strategies that produced high results that were not addressed in his meta-analysis, which will be shared.

Abbey and I were relentless and focused on changing the lives of our students and refused to curtail our efforts. A quote from John Maxwell states, *"Each day is an unrepeatable miracle. Today will never happen again, so we must make it count."* Each day had to be intentional toward our mission of increasing each student more than one year's growth in one year's time. I wanted to make sure the foundation built was indeed correct, and the ship was sailing toward the Mastery Island.

"*I can't raise the bar for others if I haven't raised the bar for myself!*"

Chapter Four

Mastery-Based Learning: In the Classroom

"Don't wait for extraordinary opportunities. Seize common occasions and make them great. Weak men wait for opportunities. Strong men make them" - Orison Swett Marden

When my principal approached me about joining him in this journey, I was honored, but intimidated. I knew that this Math Mastery Initiative IM³ in mathematics was the change that I needed to make professionally to help improve my students' math abilities. I knew it would be a big undertaking on my part, and this came into my life at the same time that my husband and I found out we were expecting our first child. It seemed like the odds were against me to begin a new teaching style, when I already knew I would have to be out of my classroom for six weeks during the school year.

Jack has always specialized in math, and this was going to be my first school year teaching a self-contained classroom and instructing students in all content areas. I had always been the third grade-reading teacher in our building, therefore taking on math was a new, intimidating obstacle for me. I began thinking that mastery could be my route to making this new journey a successful one. Math was a constant area of difficulty for our students and I wanted to make it a success. Our students deserved it!

I realized that there was no better time to implement mastery teaching in math than now. I was tackling a new content area, why not invest my energy into becoming the best math instructor I could be!

I knew my workload would increase and it would cause me to work more hours at school, but I was determined to see more growth than I had been seeing from my students. I was finding that I was more tired than my students when I was leaving work each day. If I was doing my job in an effective way, they should have been the tired ones!

Looking At Our Building Scores

As a building, we had been at a standstill with our test scores. We had seen small gains, but we felt the gains should be greater with how hard we were working. We were provided the best professional development; we worked together as a staff to share ideas and strategies, yet we were still not able to figure out how to raise our math scores. We already had an incredible team of motivated, driven educators, and we expected more from ourselves. We continued to hear from our principal, "Work smarter, not harder", but we could not make it all come together. I personally felt like, as a school, we were letting our students down. We would see their math scores at the end of every school year. I knew that we needed to make a change. I needed to know that I was helping my students reach their full potential. It was at this point I began to really dig deeper into understanding mastery teaching.

With The Third Grade Reading Guarantee (TGRG) in Ohio, my students were showing growth on the state tests, but it was never enough to be considered proficient. I hated that "passing the test" had become a goal for my students to reach by the end of the year. With state requirements, if a student does not pass the reading assessment, they are required to attend summer school. If a student takes the test during summer school and again does not pass, they are required to repeat the third grade, if they have not been previously retained. Amazing that one test puts so much pressure on these children. Passing the test was necessary. This was a goal that very few of my learners were able to achieve, and I felt terrible not fully embracing and celebrating the success the students were making over the course of the school year simply because they were not considered proficient on what the state considered to be an assessment of their learning.

I wanted to find a way to truly monitor and watch the growth of my learners, in a way we could celebrate in our classroom, to see the gains students were making. Mastery would be the way to do that!

How Did I Begin?

Every learner is different and their learning opportunities should be designed in a unique way that will benefit them. To begin implementing Math Mastery-Based Learning IM³, I knew I could not begin with both core content areas, reading and mathematics, as both content areas would take a great deal of time and dedication with this new Math Mastery Based Initiative IM³. After talking with Jack, we decided to begin with math as it is more a step-by-step process, and a way we would be able to track quicker results. Reading and writing would be more subjective, and take more time from a grading standpoint. Math was a way students could begin to see success more quickly and build their confidence within the classroom. I felt like mastery was an educational lifestyle for these students. Over the course of the year, students developed into self-motivated, determined students. If this change happened from doing mastery in mathematics, these traits would carry over into all content areas. Mastery would help build better learners, and assist with improvement with the mathematical practice of attending to precision. It empowers students to ask for clarification on their own versus waiting for feedback on a graded assignments.

We all know 3rd grade reading is a huge focal point right now. Jumping into Mastery-Based with Mathematics as my focus, did not mean I could let my reading instruction slip. I started by taking the weeks prior to the start of the school year to design a schedule that would benefit the learning I was hoping to accomplish. I knew that I needed a healthy part of my day to revolve around reading instruction. Students come to me below grade level, therefore I typically need 2-hours of reading instruction daily to ensure that we can help students make the necessary gains that will help them reach grade level potential and above.

By having reading for 2 hours daily, I am able to instruct whole group for a short time, but also incorporate guided reading groups and Daily 5 Center rotations that help students work on skills that are important to their individualized learning experiences. My main focus areas in reading are: reading fluency, reading comprehension, vocabulary and writing. Without growth in these focus areas, students will not be able to become independent learners in the years to come. On the next page is a sample schedule of how my reading block is typically set up.

Sample 3rd Grade Reading Block

30 minutes	Individualized vocabulary instruction – This is the time where I cover words revolving around our class novel or reading passages. Using different research-based strategies to better understand tier-2 and tier-3 vocabulary words.
30 minutes	Whole group reading time – During this time we work on reading our whole class novel or informational texts. We work on comprehension strategies and this is where we focus on covering whole group 3rd grade reading standards.
25 minutes	Guided Reading / CAFÉ Style Groupings – During this time, students are working in small groups that have been either assigned by teacher, or have been selected by student choice. Work is all at student's independent and instructional level to promote success and being able to complete tasks without assistance.
35 minutes	English Language Arts and Writing Block – During this time we focus on English Language Arts as well as writing. We work on parts of speech, language skills, speaking and listening, and writing. Much of our time is spent with students writing paragraph responses that relate to our class novel or informational texts read in class to prepare for state testing requirements.

Diving Deeper In Mathematics

Now that we knew we were transitioning to mastery in mathematics - we needed to break down our plan and how to begin. When thinking of how to begin, I realized that I could not begin on the first day of school. It would take time over the summer months to prepare. The first thing I decided to begin with was approaching the second grade teachers in our building and began looking at my roster of students. I have never been one to "pre-judge" a student before I had the opportunity to get to know them myself, but in this instance, the more I knew about my students, the better prepared I would be when planning our upcoming year together.

Over the summer months, I researched mastery instruction and how to instruct in a way that would promote this high level of learning for my learners. I read books, blogs and articles about various types of instruction. I met with Jack to plan for the year and map out how to begin implementation in a way that I would be able to manage on my own. I decided that I would take this first year of mastery as my learning period and make time to self-reflect and assess what I was doing right, and what needed to be changed.

I began by studying the math standards myself and becoming familiar with every math standard and what students would be learning over the course of the school year. I created a filing cabinet where every standard had its own folder, and I began to research these math standards and fill the folder with lessons and activities that I would be able to use throughout the year. This was a big job, but one that was necessary to stay organized and prepared.

I started with math power standards and built up those file folders first; I knew from researching the standards and previously summative state tests that these standards were paramount in the learning progression of my students. In the file folders, I was adding sample lesson plans, anchor charts containing various teaching strategies, mastery quizzes and center ideas. I was keeping a record of which strategy I was using to teach each standard to see if they were effective and should be continued or if I needed to readjust.

During this time, I also worked on creating a pre-assessment that I would administer to students at the start of the school year to assess their current understanding of math skills. The assessment covered second and third grade standards, therefore I would be able to see common trends and misconceptions about material they may have lost or forgot over the summer months.

Once I organized these materials, I felt that I finally had a better understanding of how the year would look. I felt prepared for the instruction and implementation. However, a teacher can be the most prepared person in the world, and plans will all change once the students arrive. I needed to meet my students, get to know my group of learners, and give the pre-assessment before I could truly implement Mastery-Based Learning in Mathematics IM^3.

Using My 90-Minutes Wisely

Because we wanted to begin this implementation full time, I needed to design a schedule that would allow me to have the necessary amount of time for my math instruction. Ultimately, I had 90 minutes a day for math instruction, and although I could have used more time – I had to work with what I had. By having 90 minutes a day, I would break down my time into smaller instructional blocks. I would need time to instruct students whole group while also leaving time available for center rotations where I would be better able to focus on student's individual needs.

30 minutes	Spiral Mathematics (building-wide) Curriculum
	This is something the students in our building complete daily. It consists of one 15-question lesson each day. This is a spiral review that goes over previously taught standards, introduces grade-level standards, and previews skills for the upcoming grade at the end of the year. Each day students have 15 minutes to complete one lesson independently. After the 15 minutes is up, we spend 15 minutes as a whole class going over every question and I provide students with solutions for how to solve. I, as a teacher, track every single questions for every student - therefore I am able to better recognize trends and misconceptions. This helps when mapping out which standards to cover in which order.
30 minutes	Whole Group Math Instruction –
	During this time we focus on current grade level standards. I choose the Common Core State Standards, and then identified the power standards (previously mentioned) and provide direct instruction over these standards to introduce and practice as a class. Typically we cover one skill a week, however that is adjusted based on how much time students require to grasp the skill. Heavier covered standards will require more time, and some skills, like multiplication and division, never really go away.

30 minutes	Guided Math Centers - During this time, students are working in small intervention groups to practice skills they are struggling to master. This takes much planning on the teacher's part, but is the most important, individualized time of our day. Students will be seen around the room working in various centers. The centers are all assigned to students based on their individual needs. Observers will typically see students working on individualized computer programs, working in small groups with peers or the teacher, and some students practicing skills independently. Free online math resources are available and should be used to boost math skills and fact fluency within the classroom!

Summary

    To make math mastery possible you need to begin by taking the time to dig deeper to understand your content standards, and find the best way for you to stay organized in your work. As a Navigator, passion is paramount to making mastery a successful endeavor. Mastery works. The evidence is behind it. But the passion and organization are the foundations necessary for success.

    Everyone may start at a different point when implementing this initiative. I am confident that whatever level of implementation you begin with that you will see results and the confidence of our students will improve. This truly is a culture changing imitative that you can implement.

Chapter Five

Building a Positive Classroom Culture

When school began in August, my main focus was building a classroom environment that revolved around trust and respect for one another. Not only did I expect my students to respect me as their educator, I expected the students to respect one another so they felt our classroom was a safe place for learning to occur. Learning new material is hard and can be intimidating. There are always the students who "know everything" and new content seems to always come easy to them, and that is great. But I also wanted those struggling students to feel comfortable making mistakes and being able to ask for help when needed, even if I was not the person who they'd approach for help.

I never wanted my students to feel rushed. Sometimes mastering a skill will take a long time and many different approaches before it sticks.

Inspired by having a classroom culture that motivated my students to do their best, I stuck with the PBIS framework that Jack previously mentioned, as well as the Responsive Classroom training our district provided for our building. I decided it was important to spend every morning together as a class, getting to know one another and learning to accept our peers. This time was known as our morning meeting, and it quickly became the most influential piece of our school day.

Social Emotional Learning; SEL

Social Emotional Learning (SEL) is the process through which children and adults acquire and effectively apply the knowledge, attitudes, and skills necessary to understand and manage emotions, set and achieve high positive goals, feel and show empathy for others, establish and maintain positive relationships, and make responsible decisions.

Isn't that what every teacher would strive for in a classroom? Students who believe in the content they are taught, understand why these skills are important, have positive attitudes about their learning, know how to set personal educational goals for themselves and can know when decisions can benefit their learning.

I know that SEL is a huge contributor to why my students are able to live in a high crime, high violence area, yet still come to school daily and respect one another and myself as their teacher. In our building, every teacher is SEL trained and strives to implement SEL lessons and strategies into their classrooms to make practices such as cooperative learning and project-based learning possible.

As Jack mentioned in chapter 3, as a building we have a strong focus on safety. Our surrounding area is dangerous, and that is the everyday life that our students are used to experiencing. SEL strategies focus on creating a learning environment that is safe and help our learners focus on their education during the school day.

Morning Meetings

One component of SEL, that I find to be most beneficial, is my morning meeting time. Every morning, my students arrive to school and begin unpacking their belongings. After unpacking, children work on morning work until we are ready to begin our day. Attendance issues are a huge problem with our learners, therefore beginning right when the bell rings is not beneficial to my schedule. Too many students would miss instructional time if I began right at the bell.

Shortly after morning work, my students and I would circle up in our classroom and begin our morning meeting. **Morning meetings are portioned into four different parts: The Greeting, Sharing, Activity and Morning Message.** I implement a morning meeting daily to provide consistency with my learners. This is a way to help students feel safe and build security within our four walls. If we ever have an adjusted schedule, we will always make time for our morning meeting because I believe it is extremely important in my classroom and making my students feel comfortable to come out of their shells.

The Greeting:

When facilitating a morning meeting, I begin by partnering my students with a classmate who is next to them on either side. I do the pairing to ensure students are not working with the same partner daily. Once students have been paired, we begin with our greeting. Students are taught how to greet one another properly. This is a lifelong skill, but also teaches students how to be more confident in their speaking and will lead to stronger conversational skills when speaking to adults.

A typical greeting was having students turn and face one another, and begin with a high five, handshake, or fist pump. Students were then expected to spread out throughout the room (quickly) to welcome their partner to school and give them a compliment. I also participated in these partner greetings and was intentional on which students I paired with. A greeting lasted about 1-2 minutes.

The Sharing:

After having the one-on-one time with their partner, we would regroup back to our class circle and I would assign a partner discussion question. Discussion questions can be team-building questions, for example, "What do you think is the best dinner that your mom makes?" They can also be deeper-thinking questions like, "After reading Stone Fox and Bluish, state two similarities between the two novels." After students answer these discussion questions with their partner, all pairs report back to the circle to share out. The next step is sharing out. When we conduct our share out section, I have partners share for each other. This helps the students who are introverted to build confidence in speaking out in front of others, because they are sharing what someone else stated, not their own opinion. This is also a good technique for restating the questions that are asked. My students have also always struggled with summarizing what they hear or read. This forces students to listen to learn, because they know they have to come back and share out to the class. We always begin the year with the more surface-level questions, and continue to develop to the deeper-level thinking as the year progresses.

The Activity:

Once we have done the question portion of the morning meeting, it is time to move to the activity portion of our meeting. I feel that the activity portion of the morning meeting is important to give students a chance to interact with one another in a way that is non-academic and where students can begin to build friendships and laugh together. I have used resources for various engaging activities such as:

1. *The Morning Meeting Book* 3rd Edition by Roxann Kriete and Carol Davis
2. *The First Six Weeks Of School* 2nd Edition by Roxann Kriete and Paula Denton
3. *80 Morning Meeting Ideas* for grades k-2 by Susan Lattanzi Roser

Activities should be very easy to implement, require very few materials (if any at all), and be short in length. An example of an activity I implemented during morning meeting was the Alphabet game. We could play alphabet in two different ways. One was being able to allow students to say any word that began with their letter. For the letter B, students could say balloon, broccoli, or basketball. This is an example of a non-categorical game. Or, I could assign a category for the students to add rigor to the classroom. An example of this was when we finished reading *Mouse and the Motorcycle*. Students had to state a word that related to the novel that fit the letter that was assigned to them. This gave students the idea that they were playing a game, but it also got students thinking and recalling past knowledge. Another important rule for this game was that if a student needed help coming up with a word – they were able to choose a friend to brainstorm with who was on either side of them in the circle. This continued to build the positive, encouraging environment I was striving for.

Math Activity for Morning Meeting:

For the activity portion of our morning meetings, sometimes we play games that work on content we are studying. We were focusing on learning new multiplication strategies to help us begin multiplying. We had been working on making equal groups, arrays, skip counting and using repeated addition. This specific day we were working on repeated addition and skip counting. I had two large foam dice in the middle of our circle and we were practicing multiplying by 2s. Students all got to take their shoes off to use their shoes as "2s" to skip count with.

I had one dice that was stuck on the number 2, then students took turns rolling the second dice to get our other factor for our equation. Once we had an equation built, for example, 2x4, I would choose a student to find 8 pairs of shoes to create a repeated addition sentence on the floor. They would state their repeated addition sentence to the class "2+2+2+2=8". Then, to practice skip counting, they would say, "2, 4, 6, 8".

Students were full of excitement and giggles as they took their shoes off and worked on building these repeated addition and skip counting equations. It was a silly way to start our day practicing a recently learned skill.

The Morning Message:

The final piece of a morning meeting is the morning message. Typically, teachers are taught to end their meeting with the morning message – however this order did not work for my students and our schedule. I moved the morning message to the welcome note on the board for students to see when they arrived. This gave students a chance to see what our schedule would be like for that day, and have time to read the message at their own pace the first time over. Usually, my high-achieving students would come in and read the morning message before they began to work on morning work. I knew that majority of my lower achieving students were struggling to read the message, but I needed to be sure that they were getting the encouraging note that I tried to begin their day with. Therefore, before forming our morning meeting circle each day, a student would volunteer to come to the front of the room and read the morning message. This was a good way to motivate students to learn that pre-reading was beneficial. If they wanted to read the message, which majority *do…* then students were more likely to come in and pre-read the board so they would make fewer errors when reading aloud to the class.

What I began noticing was the more routine this became – the more students were encouraged to attempt to read aloud to the class. In the beginning, all of my "strong readers" were the students whose hands were shooting up when asked to read the message. In the middle of the year, I began seeing new hands slowly going up. I was starting to see that the culture of my classroom was changing. Students began to realize that maybe they *did* have the potential to read the message. Maybe they wouldn't be teased if they made a mistake, because they were forming peer relationships. Maybe it was okay to step outside of their comfort zone.

A morning message was an easy way for me to greet my students in the morning, welcome them to school, and make them feel loved without having to take a lot of time away from completing my required duties such as; attendance, lunch count, and assisting with student morning work. My morning message was always positive and welcoming. I felt that this was a way I could help my students begin their school day with a positive mindset and set them up for success regardless of what issues they may have been dealing with before walking into my classroom. An example of my morning message can be found below:

> **Monday Sept. 18, 2017**
>
> Good morning 3rd graders! I hope you had a wonderful weekend! I missed you all and could not wait to come back to school this morning! Today we will begin our morning with morning journals, be creative and expressive in your writing! After journals, we will have our morning meeting and check in with our friends! When morning meeting ends we will have a restroom break before we begin reading. Our goal in reading today is to be better at using author's words to make inferences in our novel. After reading, we will have snack and daily 5 centers before music class. When music ends, we will have lunch and then come back for math class. This week's goal is to learn how different helpful strategies to begin learning multiplication! What an exciting week it will be! When math ends, we will have daily 3 rotations, chromebooks and then recess to finish off our day! Be kind to one another today, work hard, and be positive! I am so happy to be here with you today! <3 Mrs. Mezinko

It was about a month into the school year when I noticed that by doing classroom meetings a shift in my classroom began. My students and I had begun creating an environment where they felt safe and ready to challenge themselves with the rigorous teaching-style that I needed to implement to get them not only on track, but proficient and beyond on state testing.

Year after year, I am complimented by administration and colleagues on how well behaved my students are. I never really know *why* my students behave as well as they do, but I do know that I treat my students with the same respect I expect them to give me. A teacher cannot look at themselves as being "better" than their students. The students should look up to their educators and respect them, but we teachers need to respect our children too if we expect them to *want* to learn from us. I think our morning meetings, responsive classroom training, and PBIS framework are reasons for the respect that flows through my classroom.

Summary

Now that you have started mastery, one of the most important pieces of the puzzle is building a classroom environment where students feel safe and strive to be their best. To achieve the results you wish to get from mastery learning, the students must recognize that everyday is just as important as the last. Greeting students at the door with a smile, having positive morning meetings, and treating one another with respect and kindness is key for creating a culture where students are willing to be themselves and become confident learners.

As a Math Mastery educator, continuing to improve your pedagogy is an ongoing process. As you are asking your students to become masters of each math standard, continue to challenge yourself with implementing new evidence based practices into your instruction. As educators strive to be a "master" of all teaching standards and must continually strive to implement better strategies allowing students greater depth of content.

Chapter Six

Mastery Criteria In the Classroom

Jack and I had numerous conversations about the success criteria expected for students to reach mastery. We decided that for mastery to occur, students must earn an 85% or higher on their math post-assessments.

<u>Keep in mind, mastery was supposed to be a challenge to reach - and we did not expect every student to reach mastery levels for every standard.</u>

Jack and I looked at what scores students needed to reach to be considered proficient on our Ohio State Math Test. Students needed to answer about 70% of questions correctly to be considered proficient. We would be ecstatic if students were proficient, but by pushing our learners to always aim for 85% accuracy, students should be able to go beyond proficient, and reach accelerated and advanced on state testing. That is why, in our classroom, 85% was considered mastery, and meant students had an advanced understanding of the math content. Our goal was to advance the knowledge of our learners in mathematics. By improving their mathematical understanding we knew it would create lifelong learners who could be successful with all math content and curriculum.

Motivating Students to Become Math Masters

Now that we had success criteria established, I needed to do my part as a classroom motivator to get my students on board. As a class, we brainstormed what being a mastery level learner meant or looked like in the classroom or in the world. Many students said they considered Lebron James a master of basketball, Taylor Swift a master of singing, and Cristiano Ronaldo a master of soccer. This was a way to introduce a difficult concept to third graders in a way they would find meaningful to them.

Next, students helped in creating student-led definitions of what mastery is and we decided on a class definition. We posted our definition on the wall above our door - **to motivate us to always work hard so we will become masters.** I decided to make our first math mastery skill one that students had already learned (a review of a second grade standard) to help build confidence in their abilities and make students feel successful.

I want to be clear that mastery is NOT spending time focusing on past standards - that is typically where we would implement interventions. However, this early in the school year, during a time of review, I felt this was an acceptable way to begin the process for our classroom.

How Do State Assessments Relate to Mastery

A teacher's goal, or mine personally, is to help build successful, independent learners. However, in today's world, schools and students are judged by the state assessments.

I never wanted to be a teacher who "taught to the test". In college, I would always tell people who asked why I got into teaching it was my goal and always has been to show my students that learning can be fun. That is still my drive every morning when I wake up!

I needed to first learn my curriculum before I could begin, and then narrow down my power standards. In Ohio, The Ohio Department of Education website (ODE) is a great website that breaks down the math standards for you and shows you the percentage of each skill required of students on the test. This was how I began to map out my year for mathematics.

Once I found out which standards would be a major focus for the state assessments, I had to then take the time to organize the standards in sequential order of how I planned to teach them to students. I obviously could not teach multiplication before addition and subtraction with regrouping. It simply would not make sense. I did extensive research personally, as a first year math teacher, to see how students best comprehend math material. Jack made a good point when discussing how to begin implementation. He explained what students would be cognitively prepared to learn throughout a school year. Skills like elapsed time require more in-depth thinking and use more prior math knowledge. This is where I needed to lean on Jack and colleagues to assist me as a new math instructor.

Having your year roughly mapped out is a great start, and something I recommend doing in the months leading up to the beginning of the school year. This leaves time when school begins to dedicate your time to building those new relationships with your students. After my year was *very* roughly planned, I went back to my file folders, looked at my content I created, and made sure it aligned with the lessons I would be teaching. I also knew that now I needed to spend more time creating my mastery math assessments for all levels. Student would progress to new skills at various times, and I needed to be ready!

Every standard would be covered over the course of the year, and every standard would need level 1, level 2 and level 3 assessments. On top of that, students do NOT typically pass the mastery quiz on their first attempt, so it was extremely important to have various assessments for each math standard we would cover.

Setting Up Your Plan

For me, having a routine in place prior to implementation was key for my own personal success. I needed to have success criteria prepared for my students, but also needed to be realistic that not all students would achieve mastery after one lesson. I created a flowchart to help me stay authentic and follow the process that I believed would help my students achieve mastery.

To begin implementation, I began with introducing the new math focus skill and teaching a mini math lesson over that skill. Sometimes students know a skill, but need a refresher before being given a pre-test. After the introduction lesson, I would give the pre-test. This was a way for me to gauge how much time was needed for teaching this skill. If I had 17/20 students pass the level 1 pretest, I knew I would not need to spend a large amount of time creating centers and interventions around this skill. If 2/20 students passed the pretest, that told me that I would now need to find strategies to teach my students that had the greatest effect size, and centers that would promote mastery.

After the pretest, I would group students based on ability. These groups would be designed based off of the pretest. It was not based on score, lowest to highest. It was based on students who had similar mistakes. For example, if a student struggled with rounding to the nearest hundred, but had no mistakes in rounding to the nearest ten, they would be grouped together. This was helpful for me, because I was then able to create worksheets, centers, and personalized computer assignments that would focus only on the skill they needed to practice, not a skill they've already mastered.

After preparing my groups and their center work, we would spend 2-3 days working in these centers. Every group would work with the teacher at least once. During our time together we would have guided math lessons where we would solve problems step-by-step. We would also solve problems out loud, giving students a chance to think aloud with their peers and better understand the steps needed to reach success. By verbalizing out loud, students would be more likely to remember the steps when working independently.

After spending 2-3 days working on guided math and independent centers, students who did not pass the level 1 assessment originally would have the opportunity to try again! More often than not, with the given small group centers and re-teaching methods, students usually would improve their original score. The majority of the time they even reached the mastery score! However, some students would continue to struggle and that was the point where I would provide more intense interventions for those students. They would be taught different strategies, incase the original strategies did not make sense to them. They also would have more one-on-one time with the teacher, rather than small group. I would design homework that related directly to this skill for them. I paired them with a mentor or volunteer for more practice opportunities.

For the remainder of the students who had already met mastery, we would now move on to deeper thinking questions and prepare for level 2 and level 3 mastery assessments. I would pair students of similar ability levels and let them work together to solve practice questions. This allowed students to share their thinking with peers and gave them practice time for solving challenging problems before solving them independently on a mastery quiz. This process continued for every 3rd grade power standard that was covered. I used these steps for every math domain and strand.

The challenging part of mastery is staying organized. You need to be sure that you are prepared for all standards prior to beginning implementation because you WILL have students who progress quicker than others. The point of mastery is allowing students to progress at their own pace and not holding high learners back. Therefore, before school begins, I would recommend creating a math filing cabinet for mastery.

If you followed the preparing steps, created your filing cabinet and made folders for all content and lessons, you are ready for the next step. The next step I would recommend is creating or locating various versions of assessments for each level or standard. The reason for needing various versions is that when learning new material, some students will struggle and may need several opportunities. If you always give the same level 1 quiz, students may begin to memorize the answers and then it will not be a true assessment of their knowledge.

I have always been told that it is effective to have students retest, but being new to mastery, I did not know if retesting would benefit or hinder the learning process. I read the book *Learning To Love Math* by Judy

Willis, M.D., and came across several pieces of research that I used to help me become more confident in my decision to allow students multiple attempts at mastery. She wrote, *"Retests provide opportunities to reevaluate answers and make corrections, as necessary. To ensure mastery, I require that students take a retest when they score under 85 percent. My primary goal is to have students learn the appropriate material so they can move forward with an adequate background for success."* This made me realize that by providing interventions, making time to conference with students, and giving students specific feedback after assessments, retesting would benefit the learner throughout the mastery process.

After coming across Dr. Willis' research, I knew, I need to be prepared for the testing process. By having various versions of assessments for each skill, it was a way for me to know when to take a "break" from a skill and move on to something new. This can help you better track when a student is becoming burned out. If I had a student attempt a rounding mastery quiz five times, I would know they need a break. I would then introduce them to a new skill, and come back to rounding at another time. Mastery should be something students are motivated by, not something that tears them down.

Another very crucial part of mastery instruction is providing specific feedback to your learners so that they are able to make changes and succeed with more practice. If a student continues to take mastery assessments, and are not given specific feedback, they will not know where their mistakes are taking place. If a student is struggling with 3-digit addition with regrouping and do not realize that they have to carry to the next place value, they will continue to get questions wrong. They need to be shown how to correct their mistakes. Without feedback, students may not be able to ever reach mastery for a skill.

"If students are to become active evaluators of their own progress, teachers must provide the students with appropriate feedback so that they can engage in this task." - John Hattie

A Closer Look at Leveled Assessments

Level 1 Mastery Assessment

A level 1 mastery assessment, as Jack and I decided, would be your regular in class questions. Many of these questions would be straightforward and usually single step problems. Sometimes these questions may even be multiple-choice questions. The purpose of a level 1 assessment is to quickly assess a student's basic understanding of a new, specific, grade-level skill. After teaching a unit on rounding, I gave students a 12-question assessment. On the assessment, there were 6 questions where students were given numbers and they were asked to round the given number to the nearest 10. The final 6 questions, students were asked to round the given number to the nearest 100. This is nothing new, or unheard of in the teaching world – this just sounds like a simple assessment, and it is. However, when we come to grading is where I was able to see if a student would reach mastery. As mentioned previously, 85% or higher is what Jack and I expected from our students. On a 12-question assessment, that meant students were only able to miss one question to be considered a master with that skill. That is a challenging assessment for a student who just learned a new skill if you ask me!

If a student earned a score of 10 out of 12, or lower, that student was not considered proficient, under my classroom expectation, and would not earn mastery for that skill. What I would do next for those students would be to begin implementing interventions and small group work for the students who were not reaching our mastery level. I implemented these interventions, during our daily computer time.

What Qualifies as a Level 2 or Level 3 Assessment?

Level 2 and level 3 assessments have the same requirements and expectations as a level 1 assessment, with more rigorous questioning techniques. As stated above, level 1 questions are your basic surface level questions for a student to answer. Level 2 and level 3 questions are more lengthy questions that typically take more time and thought to be able to solve. Level 2 questions should take your learners more time to complete and a level 2 assessment may have fewer questions than a level 1 since they will require more thinking.

Resources that I use as level 2 assessments and/or inspiration to create my own level 2 assessments, would be websites like www.engageny.org. This website has their printables organized by standard, and are challenging, multi-step questions like I was looking for. There were times that I created my own mastery assessments, but I also took advantage of the resources that were available to me. Don't recreate the wheel. Use resources that are strong and effective. Researching the resources you plan to use is extremely important. Use materials that meet the high rigor expectations you expect for your children.

Level 3 assessments should be most difficult for your class of learners. It should be a very high achieving goal and not every student may reach level 3. Some students may never pass a level 3 assessment during the year, however I will continue to provide interventions and the necessary resources until the end of the school year. I had several students with learning disabilities that were unidentified for majority of the school year.

Some of those students never passed a level 3 assessment, but they did reach mastery at either level 1 or level 2. It is important to remember that it's ok, and not every student will learn at the same pace. **That is the point of teaching students in a mastery setting!**

Classroom Assessments

I began this process by taking time to introduce the skill we would be focusing on first as a class - addition and subtraction with regrouping. This was a 2nd grade skill, but it is where our curriculum map begins the year - to review previous material and get student refocused after the "summer slide". We began our introduction to this standard as whole class instruction. Throughout the unit, we began to break apart and work in small groups based on the amount of support students needed to be successful. After working on this skill for 1-2 weeks time, I let students know we would have our first "Mastery Quiz". Students were excited and eager to know if they would be the "first" math master.

I prepared a 12 question post-assessment with equations where students would be adding and subtracting two and three digit numbers that would require regrouping. This would be considered a "level 1 assessment" with straight-forward questions. Level 1 questions were similar to classroom test questions that did not require much critical thinking.

Since this was a 12-question assessment, and a second grade skill, I required students to earn an 11/12 on their post-assessment to be considered reaching mastery for this standard. Before giving the post-assessment, we discussed how mastery is not meant to be an easy accomplishment and it is meant to be a process that takes time. I also reminded students that some skills require more time and focus in order for them to reach mastery. I worked hard at <u>introducing mastery as a positive</u>

way of learning, and not something students should be upset about if mastery was not met on an assessment.

After our first round of instruction, interventions and master assessment, we were able to start celebrating the success of the learners who reached level 1 mastery for that standard!

We started a mastery wall in our classroom which would keep track of which students have mastered each standard. This wall was a very simple way for students to manage their own growth and skill development. I began by using a chart that had every third grade math standard posted across the top of the chart, with a short description of that standard. For example, 3.nbt.1 rounding to 10s and 100s. Student names went down the left hand side. In each math standard column, there were three boxes. These boxes had a 1, 2, or 3 in it. These would help me identify which level of that standard a student had mastered. This also helped students recognize the skill they learned and displayed the standard using correct terminology. It was a good way for a guest to enter our classroom, and visually see how my students were progressing. When Jack would enter the room, he was able to comment on learners who were improving and gaining mastery slower than others and build up their confidence.

It is no secret that students always enjoy something "extra". Sometimes seeing their name on a wall is enough, but my students seemed to crave more of an incentive to motivate them. I did not want to give students candy for their success, although that may have been enough for third graders. I wanted a way to reward students in a positive way. Some teachers or principals may not support the reward concept, therefore I dug deeper for something to support my feelings. I did not want my students to be motivated for a day. I needed their long term buy in, therefore I would need something bigger to push them. Dr. Judy Willis wrote, *"The intrinsic rewards of solving challenging problems are powerful, and the dopamine-pleasure reaction encourages subsequent similar pursuits. From authentic achievements with suitable challenges, students experience the rewards of their competence, effort, and perseverance. Once this happens, math negativity declines and resilience builds. Students see themselves as learners and inventors of math."* I then realized students do not need candy, pencils, stickers or a random high-five. They wanted to be recognized for being smart. They wanted to be noticed for solving challenging math problems. They wanted to be pushed harder.

That is when I came up with Master-gram. I know social media is huge right now in the technologically savvy world our children are being raised in. All students are aware of Facebook and Instagram and the one focal point I wanted to focus on was the capability of getting "likes" on these platforms.

I decided to create a Master-gram feed for our classroom and hung it outside of my classroom door to display for others to see. I created an Avatar on www.avatarmaker.com and it was completely free. I made my avatar to look as much like me as I could. I posted my name above the avatar, and then below the avatar there are various levels of "likes". Students would soon be able to earn likes for the amount of skills they master.

Mrs. Mezinko

Level 1 Skills Mastered: ♥
Level 2 Skills Mastered: ♥
Level 3 Skills Mastered: ♥

During the first week of mastery, when I was introducing mastery, I allowed students to also go on Avatar Maker to create their own avatar to resemble themselves too. I then edited their avatar, and added their name above their avatar and hearts below the image. The hearts below the avatar represent "likes" similar to Instagram. These likes will be given every time a student masters a skill. The three levels of hearts are for level 1, 2 and 3 mastery levels. As students master more skills, I will also have a trending student of the week, who is the learner with the most skills mastered.

Level 1 Skills Mastered: ♥

Level 2 Skills Mastered: ♥

Level 3 Skills Mastered: ♥

    Another way to keep students motivated is by including staff and administrators to celebrate student success. I reached out to our entire staff during a staff meeting and explained the purpose of the avatars on my poster. I asked all teachers, administration, and building staff to periodically take time to "notice" my student's avatars and ask them about why they were wearing them. This would help keep students excited to show off their learning, but would also hold the students accountable for explaining what skills they had mastered in math. The students felt proud when junior high teachers and students would question their skills, and they were able to **brag about their learning for a change!**

The excitement the day that I hung the mastery wall was incredible! The students were so excited to see the Mastergram feed, and to check their own status. It took me very little time, money and preparation to accomplish. If you look at the photograph above, student's names were above their avatar, then their photo, and at the bottom are the 3 tiers of mastery next to the hearts which represent "likes". Every time a student mastered a skill, I changed their number of likes. They were very motivated by this and wanted to compete with their peers to master more skills.

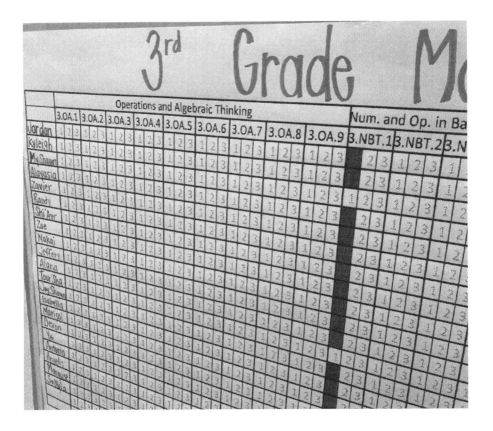

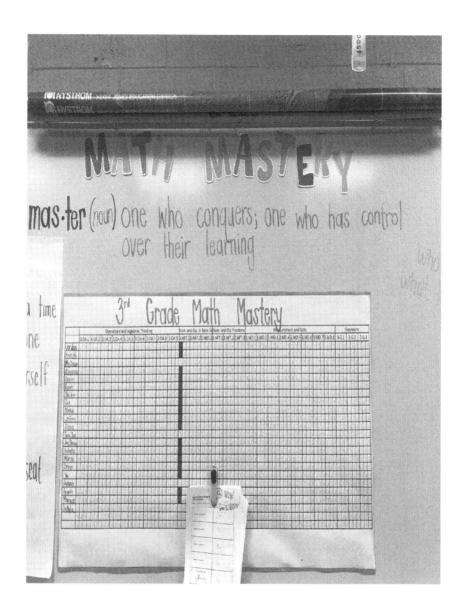

As we began to master this first skill, we moved on to more challenging third grade standards. Each week I had been introducing a new standard and I had been following the process mentioned above in guiding students to reaching mastery in these skills. Some more complex standards do require more time, and not all standards can be covered in a week's timeline. Be open-minded and aware of your students needs when deciding how long to spend instructing on a new skill. Some skills will come easy to your learners, and some will take a great deal of time and instruction.

Now that I had been implementing mastery since early-September, an entire wall of our classroom was covered with skills we had learned and names of students who have mastered those skills. All students had mastered two or more standards. Some students began working on mastering those standards at level 2 or level 3, which dig deeper into more critical thinking questions for each standard. I began to truly notice my learners taking ownership over their learning. The most precious part of mastery to me, was that even my students who were un-identified with learning disabilities (later identified in the year) were mastering these skills. It was NOT the content, it was the process and taking the time to connect with *every* student in a way that was meaningful to them. It meant never giving up on my students. I worked on different strategies until it made sense for them. They were becoming masters - right in front of my eyes

Implementing Our Interventions

Mastery sounds like the perfect plan, and in my eyes, it is. But not all students can master every skill with ease. Many skills will take a lot of practice and patience to learn. We have to remember that these skills are all new to students. These are new concepts that students are unfamiliar with. So, as teachers, we cannot expect that all skills come easily to students. There will be learners who struggle, and it is our job to keep them in a positive mind frame so they will be able to master the challenges they face with the proper interventions.

When implementing interventions, I would group students with similar struggling areas. I would begin by laying out all mastery quizzes on a table – and sort students into three groups. Students who struggled to round to the nearest 10, students who struggled to round to the nearest 100, and students who did not seem to understand rounding at all. These three groups were then divided into smaller groups as deemed necessary. For example, if a student missed every question – they would require re-teaching of the skill as a whole. But if a student maybe struggles with 1-2 questions on rounding to the nearest hundred, I would pull them to my back table, work on several problems with the student, assign bonus homework that night which would practice that skill, and then see if the student progresses.

For students who did not reach mastery – they were required to attend at least one intervention session before attempting another mastery quiz on that individual skill. I would keep all original quizzes and then write the date in which they attended the intervention session; therefore I would be able to easily track when they were able to have another attempt. This process was one that worked for me, but you could easily create a spreadsheet or another tracking method that works for you! This requirement of attending an intervention time helped slow my reactive students, and made them take time to practice the skill before trying again. I did not want students trying to pass a mastery quiz daily and continue failing because they have not had the proper amount of time to relearn or practice the skill. This would lead to frustration and students who would become non-believers. Students began the mastery process being very eager to "try again", and I needed to show my students the importance of time and expressing that learning a skill that they will remember and retain, takes practice and patience.

What about the "Non-Believer" Students

Success stories are powerful, and really give me a chance to reflect on my journey of flipping my classroom. Looking back, not every student was as excited as the students mentioned above. I did not have students who absolutely refused to buy-in to the thought of mastery. But I did have students who seemed nervous about the idea.

I have a feeling that student excitement was due to the way it was introduced and presented to them. I was genuinely excited as a teacher - therefore my students sensed my excitement and were eager to begin. I have the advantage of being a teacher of younger children, but I am a firm believer that students strive to please their educators. If I was excited, they wanted to be excited with me.

I anticipated student frustration and their lack of background knowledge on some specific areas, however I allowed them to struggle to demonstrate the need for perseverance and for finding different methods for learning the content. The classroom culture was such that even when students wanted to give up their classmates provided extra support for when they began to struggle and reach frustration on a topic.

Students had always been instructed whole group up until this point in their schooling. They never had to challenge themselves to answer rigorous questions - and surely they never felt the need to push themselves and compete to keep up with their peers. When students earned good grades before, it was always enough. *But now, earning "good grades" was a thing of the past.* They needed to master skills and show that they understood concepts. I incorporated the Habits of Mind that our building had adapted, and taught students how to always stay positive and determined. I did not want to bring students down, I wanted to build them up.

It was at this point that students were realizing the challenge I had presented to them. They started to realize that when they *did* master skills - they were pushed to master that same skill at a higher level. The learning never stopped.

It was no longer the smartest students who were the most successful - it was the hardest workers, the most motivated!

As this happened, the classroom began to flip. I was no longer teaching math class while students sat and listened - students were learning on computers, watching videos to assist with mastery, practicing skills with mentors, teaching their classroom partners how to master skills and working on computerized programs. It was no longer a traditional classroom, and it was an idea some students had a hard time adjusting to.

I needed to stay excited and motivated for my students. I would constantly report successes to Jack so that he could stop into our classroom and celebrate the math successes of the students. Many days starting out - I would send a quick text or email to him about minor successes, just to keep him visiting our classroom and keeping the students interested in reaching these new levels of learning. When students got used to seeing Mr. Hunter in our classroom, the harder they worked because they wanted to be the reason he was there. The students who wanted to give little effort slowly began to give more effort. When I noticed their interest peak - I would have small motivational moments with them. It was sometimes a quick note - "I've noticed you working really hard lately" - and other times it was a bigger investment, like inviting them to have lunch with me for a longer conversation. I cannot count how many of my lunches I "missed" in the teachers lounge so that I could eat with students instead, and those were turning points that I couldn't afford to lose.

I would always explain to my students that my passion began when I was young. I would tell them stories about myself, playing school in my childhood basement where I was the teacher - and my students were invisible. I worked hard in life, and because of the work I put in I earned the reward of being their teacher now. I explained that in life, when you work hard your dreams can come true. I always told my students that as long as they were in my class, I would never let them fail. I was never going to give up on them - even if they gave up on themselves. I would still be at work everyday. The success of math mastery provided motivational moments with my students - they all bought in to mastery learning, and they wanted to master the skills for themselves, but they also wanted to do it for me.

How Mastery Supported Classroom Management

When I refused to give in and give up on my students, the behaviors began to diminish. There were students who tried to act out. There were when days students would rip up their mastery quiz, students broke pencils, and students straight up refused to do anything. But I consistently handled the behaviors within my classroom. I did not want my students to realize if they acted out they would be able to leave the classroom as part of their punishment, I needed them in my classroom.

Since Mr. Hunter is the building principal, he typically handles referrals for students who have been asked to leave class - but I wanted my students to see Jack as a supporter and someone who believed in them, not someone who gave consequences for their actions. A few of my students were choosing to act out so that they could leave class and get away from the rigor and high expectations that I had for them. They wanted to fail because they were afraid they couldn't succeed. I was not going to let them do that. So I began to handle all (manageable) behaviors within the classroom.

I began to allow students to "take a break" when they felt overwhelmed or frustrated. I have a break station in my classroom that has a chair, pillows, lava lamp, and stress balls. Students were able to "tap out" and take a break at the break station if they felt it was necessary. At the beginning, students tried to over use the break station. But it was important to let students use it as often as they wanted. I never wanted it to become a negative place. And over time, the breaks became less and less frequent. The only rule I had was that they could only stay a couple of minutes (2-3). If a student was still not calm after that amount of time, I had an arrangement with my teaching partner, that we could send students (her students to me, and mine to her) for a 5-minute break where they were expected to complete a written reflection plan. This was a longer task and students were now expected to complete it before coming back to class. The reflection plans were typically stored in a file cabinet, but for those repeating offenders, the reflection sheets were sent home to be signed by a parent.

As students began to get more comfortable with the way our classroom was running, the behaviors began to diminish and there were fewer students needing breaks each day. Students quickly realized that poor behavior would not get them out of the classroom and to the office. The consequences would never be enough (in my eyes) for a student to lose out on their education. Once I convinced myself that their learning was the most important thing, the students began realizing that I was not giving up on them. They slowly began to believe in themselves as I believed in them.

Summary

"If a movement is to have an impact it must belong to those who join it not just those who lead it"

Simon Sinek

You are working on building up your classroom climate and now the important part of your day is working on implementing mastery in your classroom. Begin by creating hands on and engaging lessons to raise interest in the content you are teaching. Begin by giving pre assessments to gauge where student's current understanding resides. Once you teach a unit and give students time to practice their new material, mastery assessments can occur in your classroom! Get excited! This should be a time to excite your students and create your mastery wall to track their success! Remember to know when your students hit their frustration level, and give them time for more practice and interventions. Sometimes it is beneficial to stop and move on to something else before revisiting the content they were frustrated with.

Chapter Seven

"It takes a village to raise a child, find a village, encourage one another and open your village to one another"

As mentioned previously, this is a daunting task to do alone as one teacher. I was excited that Jack believed in me enough to ask me to lead this initiative and he provided continued guidance. Support from your building administration is key to being able to dig deeper with the lowest performing students. As a teacher, my job was to figure out each student's strengths and weaknesses, but then also be able to find support for those students when I was unable to work at a slower pace to benefit their learning and processing time.

Jack volunteered time at the end of every school day to pull students to the cafeteria and provide math interventions. He would reteach skills that I have flagged as concern areas for each child by direct one-on-one instruction, but also building personalized computer programs that would practice those challenging concepts. It was amazing to see progress made by these students after working with Jack. Sometimes students need a change of scenery to learn at their full potential. Most teachers, including myself, like to have all of the answers and be in control of our student's learning - but thinking outside the box and letting Jack step in and offer his support was not only helpful to me, but also my learners.

Another way I provided more individualized instruction to each child was by recruiting volunteers to come in weekly to help meet my student's needs. Jack recruited volunteers from numerous local businesses in the adjacent areas. These volunteers came to work with their assigned student one day per week, for one hour each visit. By having a routine schedule, I was able to prepare activities and games that the students would be able to do with their mentor. The mentors would review skills that were important for students to reach their personal math mastery goals. Outside of the volunteers Jack brought in, I also found family members and friends that felt strongly about helping my students and adopted a student to mentor. **There are people who feel passionately about helping children - we just need to find them!**

    I knew once I got volunteers in the door, they wouldn't want to leave! My students are infectious! By doing this, 7 of my students have one-on-one, weekly mentors. The lessons I created provided students a chance to work on their weaknesses with someone by their side helping and walking them through the problem solving strategies.

    Another resource I approached was my aunt who is a retired teacher. She shares the passion that I have for teaching and could see how desperate I was to help children reach their full potential, even if it meant a heavier workload on my part. My aunt came in once a week for 3 hours. During her time, I would have her pull small groups into the hall outside of my classroom door. These groups of students were constantly changing based on the students who struggled with the weekly concepts at that time. As mentioned before, I tried to cover standards in 1-2 weeks time. The students who were working at a slower pace would work in the hall for more practice. I would also plan some days where my high-scoring students would be a group to work with my aunt in the hall. They would be working on higher level thinking questions or mini group projects to continue to have those students reach for higher achievement. I never wanted students to feel like they always *had* to go work with a mentor. It was all about balance and finding what was most important to the students.

If you have ever heard the phrase, "It takes a village to raise a child...", I was quickly realizing that this applied for classrooms too!

At first, I felt like by inviting mentors and volunteers into my classroom meant having to give up my role as the sole instructor. But during the time I've been on this journey, I have realized that my students trust and recognize me as their instructional leader. They see these volunteers as a way for them to be able to get more help when I am unable to help every child one-on-one every day. This was a topic we had to cover as a class, and I had to explain that every student would get time with mentors, but the mentors were there for limited time, and I had to use their skills as I deemed necessary that day.

Along with valuing your volunteers, you need to be well prepared and organized. There is nothing worse than asking for someone's time, and then not being ready when they arrive! I had a small tote for each volunteer with his/her name on it. The totes are stored above my student cubbies, because, let's be honest - there is no "open space" in most classrooms! Inside each tote were the necessary materials the mentor would need for that day. Not every tote was identical, because not every child was working on the same skills. Each tote had a folder. Inside the folder were progress monitoring sheets, games, directions, or even lesson plans. I also would put a small index card inside the folder each day - identifying which student that mentor would be working with. As mentioned before, not every child saw a mentor each week - and some students saw several. This folder was a way for the volunteer to arrive to our classroom and quickly scan the day's activities before pulling their student to work with. Standard materials were also stored in each tote. The materials I provided were pencils, erasers, pens of various colors, crayons and markers, paper, a timer (for timed math fact tests or reading fluency checks), a mini clock to track time, and highlighters. There were also materials that I needed to add if a game or activity required more supplies. Some of the frequently used items were: dice, rulers, counting chips, a clock students could manipulate, a deck of cards and other math manipulatives. These items were ones I would add to the tote as needed. That is why it was important to always be prepared and ready. I am frequently asked what I did if a mentor showed up and the student they work with was absent. Easy fix: send another student that works at a similar ability level. Extra practice never hurts! Also, if a mentor was scheduled to come - there were days things would come up and they would not be able to make it. Those days, I would be honest with my students and let them know something came up and their mentor will not be there for that session. I would keep track, therefore the next time the mentor came - that student would be the first one to go work with them! My students face a lot of let downs in their lives, and I did not want mentors to become something that seemed like a let down or failure to them. It was always a positive experience, and one my students and mentors cherished.

The final topic that is important to cover with your children prior to inviting volunteers into your classroom is your expectations. When I began introducing the idea of volunteers coming into our classroom with my students - I began by explaining that volunteers commit their valuable time to help us and do not get compensation for doing so. Many of these volunteers came from our business partnership for our school - and it was important to express how many resources and opportunities they had been given from these volunteers. We made an anchor chart to display expectations of how to treat visitors. We discussed proper conversational topics, and how to speak loud enough for their volunteer to help them and to also speak clearly. It was also important to explain that students were expected to be hard workers and not argue that they "already know" the topic they may encounter. I explained that if the class expectations were not followed through, they would lose their opportunity to work with a mentor. Different ideas my students came up with are listed below:

Do not speak over adults or classmates when they speak
Work hard and listen to directions
Take your time, be neat, stay organized
Be open-minded to different learning strategies
Respect the adult, and possible classmates you are working with

---

All students committed to following these rules and signed their signature at the bottom of our anchor chart. This was a way to hold students accountable - and if a student chose to break one of the expectations, I would have a conversation with that child and refer to our anchor chart of expectations. That way I was always being fair, no rules were changing, and the expectations were the same for all students!

You can become a classroom that is driven by mastery with simply dedication and determination to see growth from your students. Keep the passion for this career alive within you, and find at least one strong person you can lean on when you feel like you are struggling.

Staying Mentally Tough: For Your Students

"Trust yourself. Create the kind of self that you will be happy to live with all your life. Make the most of yourself by fanning the tiny, inner sparks of possibility into flames of achievement." -- Golda Meir

When beginning the Math Mastery Initiative IM³, I knew there would be days where I struggled believing the progress would lead to proficiency. Finally in the beginning of December my students were required to take the Ohio MAP Test. To say that I was nervous is an understatement. I couldn't sleep the night before. I got to school even earlier than normal, and I remember walking around my room that morning before students arrived, trying to complete many tasks - yet not completing any because I just did not have focus for anything other than their scores.

The students arrived and we began our day, sticking to our normal morning routine to keep my learners from sharing the same test-day jitters that I was feeling. We had a morning meeting, used the restroom, and I gave the students a snack. I remember reading the testing directions, telling my students they may begin their tests, and saying good luck. Walking around the room, monitoring their testing screens, I noticed something. If I had to describe my classroom in one word, it would be calm. My students were not looking around the room. They were not wiggling their feet. They were not distracted and doodling on their scrap paper provided to work out challenging problems. They were working. They were focused. They were confident. It was in that moment that I realized that I had prepared them for success and had shown them how to trust that they know this content. I had been teaching them how to master their skills, but within doing that, I built independence and instilled confidence in them.

On this specific test, student scores pop up when they have completed the assessment. I had a clipboard, and as students were finishing, I was walking to their computer to write down their score. On my clipboard, I had a class list with every child's name and their fall math score. As I was writing down these new winter math scores that were rolling in, I was shocked by the numbers I was seeing. Students were improving their scores, and were earning higher scores than I had anticipated. It was in that moment that I knew, mastery was working.

I was the focus class for this study in our building and I was extremely lucky to have the support that I did. However, as I began to see growth in my students in a very short period of time, and as those winter test scores were released, Jack and I found it hard to not share our excitement and success with more educators from our team. The more others began to hear about what I was doing in my classroom, the more interest and buy in we began to see from our strongest teachers.

Fellow coworkers were stopping in my classroom to view my mastery wall, teachers were stopping my students in the hallway to ask them about their learning, and teachers who I had never collaborated with (teachers in higher grade levels) became more interested in working together to share ideas. Did we still have educators who did not take the time to listen and understand what we were doing? Of course there are Anchors and Riders in every organization. But those educators who took the time to see what we had quickly become so passionate about, also seemed to find that same passion over helping their learners reach mastery potential.

As we were creating this Math Mastery Model, IM^3 we had no reassurances that the process would yield the results we desired for our learners. Once these results became visible we knew the strategies and processes we created were going to be validated to the expectations we set forth in the beginning.

Building Curiosity amongst Staff

Quickly, we had more teachers passionate about their students learning, and the climate of our building began to change. As this journey was underway, my students shared a lot of excitement about their learning. It was impossible for other students and teachers to miss the environmental change that had taken place in my room over the first semester of the school year. The Navigators and some Aspiring Navigators on our staff wanted more information - and Jack and I wanted to help. Jack and I met prior to providing any information to interested staff and decided that we would provide guidance on implementation and the beginning planning phases of math mastery. This process takes time on the educator's part as well as training for the students in the classroom. We wanted to ensure the implementation was successful and wanted to keep a realistic timeline for the interested Navigators and Aspiring Navigators.

Math Mastery Based Learning Model IM³ was starting to show evidence of student success. Here are three evidence-based student success stories.

Student Success Story #1:
This year I had a 3rd grader who was a repeater. He was in my teaching partner's class last year - and this year he was mine! I was nervous to have him, as I was afraid he would be angry and hold a grudge that he was not

moving to 4th with all of his friends. Reading was a weakness for him, but this year math was proving to be his strong area! As we began mastery, he was better able to master skills this year. He began math mastery and showed excitement at his achievement.

At a school-wide assembly, Jack was discussing the Habits of Mind, and how using past knowledge and perseverance are key to being successful in school. Jack noticed this student sitting in the crowd and was aware of his recent achievements with math mastery. He called him up in front of the school and asked him about his recent math accomplishments. This young man took the microphone, and walked around the room, arms out addressing his audience. He explained that in our classroom, we were building math masters one standard at a time. He explained what a master was (using our classroom definition), and then went on to talk about the skills he has mastered. What was most impressive to me and the other teachers in the audience was when Jack said, "Wow! I am proud of you reaching mastery. Can you tell us what areas you have mastered? In front of the whole school, this child said with confidence, "3.nbt.1 means that I am a master at rounding 2 and 3 digit numbers to the nearest ten and hundred.... You know, like 75 would round to 80 if we were rounding to the nearest ten. 3.nbt.2 means that I can add and subtract with regrouping, I can borrow and stuff... and 3.md.1 means that I have mastered telling time on a clock and being able to figure out tough elapsed time problems."

WOAH! How powerful is that? What more in life could a teacher dream of than having their students be able to not only complete challenging problems, but truly make learning meaningful and important to them? This is how we change lives and education forever.

Student Success Story #2:

Our students live with many challenges that most people could never imagine facing in a lifetime. Many students have an unfortunate living arrangement, and it leads to chronic absences at school. This is a struggle and typically, students who miss school the most have a harder time keeping up on assignments and therefore have poorer grades.

When we began implementing mastery, I stressed the importance of being at school everyday, and being on time. As a class, we discussed how important school is and we decided to challenge ourselves to have better class attendance. We began tracking the days of school that we had perfect attendance. If a student arrived late or had to dismiss early, we would not allow this to interfere with our math mastery goals. Our main focus was to have every student at school, everyday, for 10 days.

My students can be easily motivated, usually involving small rewards. A popular reward my students choose is a popcorn party. It is an easy reward to follow through with on my end, and it is exciting enough to keep my students working toward their goals.

This year, I had one student who was _always_ absent. He was a smart child, one of my highest performing math students, but he was not progressing at the rates of his peers. There was a time when this young man missed 12 days of school in a row. My students were getting so down, realizing that without their classmate, they would not be able to earn a reward. I overheard students talking during math centers that day, and one young girl said to her friend, "You know.. Popcorn parties are cool... but (absent student) hasn't been at school in a long time, and his name is not on the mastery wall as much as everybody else. We need to get him back at school so that he can keep learning."

The next morning, I circled up my students for our daily morning meeting and our absent student was once again, absent. We began welcoming one another to school and then right as we were about to break off into partners, the door opened. In walked our classmate we had been waiting to see for 12 days! The whole class started clapping and cheering that he was at school. They began swarming him and I could see the students in my class hugging him and high-fiving him because he came to school. My students were expressing how much they had missed him and how excited they were that he was back.

We did not earn a popcorn party that day, but we did get a tally mark toward our perfect attendance reward. What was most meaningful that day to me was that when I walked my students to physical education class that day, that young man stopped before going into the gymnasium and asked if he could spend his gym time working on his math mastery work. I immediately told him yes and let him come back to the room to work on getting caught up.

I realized how important school was to this child. He did not want to be absent all the time. His friends did not want him to miss school. But sometimes our students don't have a choice. We have to work with them and help them at all possible opportunities because we don't know what challenges they are facing when we aren't around.

Student Success Story #3:

A powerful moment toward the end of the year was with one of my female students. She had mastered all 3rd grade standards at level 1, and had moved on to reaching level 2 and 3 for most standards! She was very bright and was self-motivated.

On Fridays, students who have all of their work from the week completed and turned in earn "free time Friday" for 20 minutes. This rewards the students who have worked hard all week and it gives those students who may have been absent, had missing assignments, or those needing to make corrections on low-scoring assignments time to make up their work.

During free time, this student had all of her work done and had been working independently on the district provided computer math program. She was being given 4th grade math questions and she was getting frustrated. She did not know what prime and composite numbers were, and she knew it was not a skill we would cover in class. Instead of giving up, this student came to me and asked for a mini lesson. I spent the entire 20 minutes explaining prime and composite numbers to her that day.

At the end of free time, she still was struggling. We did not have enough time to practice together for her to grasp the concept. That weekend, she went home and spent two days watching videos on how to better understand the difference between prime and composite numbers and how to identify them. On Monday, she came back and began doing her computerized program and got every single question right on prime and composite numbers.

She had learned over the course of the school year how to master skills. She attempted them on her own, practiced, asked for assistance from the educator, and then practiced the new skills independently until she was able to successfully understand the concept! She understood how to take learning into her own hands when I was not around to provide support. Learning was important to her, and she showed me that she was a master of math!

Summary

Looking back on my mastery journey, I am beaming with pride. Jack and I had many obstacles, challenges and excuses for why implementing mastery *shouldn't* have worked for us, but it did. We were a two-man team, working with inner city students who were sometimes two years below grade level. **But with our hard work, passion and dedication, we did it!** We changed the lives and educational outlook for our learners and we are creating lifelong learners. We have, together, encouraged more people within our building to experience math mastery learning and share the excitement when students succeed. Together, we have created a way for all students to reach success, and it has truly been life changing for me as an educator. I am so eager to begin year two of my mastery journey.

Steps for Preparing for Mastery

1. Learn and understand your content and standards
2. Research the power standards for your State Test
3. Put your strands in sequential order based on difficulty
4. Make a pre-test for each standard that you will cover
5. Create multiple post-tests
    - important to have many versions for each skill and each level for those students who need multiple attempts to reach mastery
6. Find your most effective strategies, supports and centers to use

Steps for Implementing Mastery

1. Introduction of one skill – whole group
2. Begin implementing small group instruction and centers
3. Give student a mastery quiz
    - If Pass: student then begins preparing for level 2
    - If Fail: student then begins re-teaching and intervention process.

Chapter Eight

The Evidence

Test Class versus Placebo

I will now delve into two similar classrooms, one in which implemented our Mastery-Based initiative using the math instructional model and the other who did not. Both classrooms have the identical number of students with baseline math scores through NWEA (Northwest Evaluation Association) assessments within 3 RIT points at the end of the previous year. NWEA defines RIT Scores as: *a **scale** to measure student achievement and growth.* ***RIT*** *stands for Rasch Unit, which is a measurement **scale** developed to simplify the interpretation of test **scores**.* Both classrooms have a similar number of students, and includes a few students identified with disabilities or who are in the process of being identified as having a disability. In our district, class lists of students are divided by the previous year's teachers and selected via a blind draw. In other words, students who were in Abbey's class were not pre-selected. It did not matter what student list Abbey inherited, she had a thorough understanding of how kids learn regardless of their background knowledge. Some of her students were in the intervention process already from the previous year and actually qualified for an IEP, however, not in math.

How We Compiled and Analyzed the Summative Data

With my background in mathematics and numerous statistics courses, I knew I could calculate the effect size of this small sample. A small sample size can cause more variance in data collection. I had to ensure the conditions in both classes were the same. I needed to ensure they had the same amount of instructional time, behavior support, resources and all other materials. This proved to create a data set that was very comparative in every area. We looked at testing conditions which were found to be identical, as both classes tested on the same day, at the same time, with the same type of media, Chromebooks. The students were all provided with mints, snacks and permitted to walk prior to the test. We use the same procedures even if not comparing classes, it's just what we do. I am informing the reader of the testing variables to further validate the data and quell the concern that one group had a distinct advantage over the other group.

Formative Assessments

We were not content betting all of our success on one district mandated quarterly assessment via NWEA. Although the data was promising, it was the short cycle assessments and the formative checks that truly showed how much the effect size increased. Abbey continued to assess her students frequently and provide data to me to calculate the effect size of the practices she was using. Mezinko would provide me with pre/post test data for her assessments and allow me to validate her assumptions. Also she would notate what strategy she used for each standard, which assisted me with calculating the effect size. I would match the calculated effect size against Hattie's list of meta-analysis to see if they were close to his research. In all instances they were within 5 percentage points.

Summative Assessments

When the fall Map Assessment was given, Mezinko's RIT score average was 189 with a standard deviation of 9.97. The non-mastery class had an average RIT score of 186 with a standard Deviation of 10.21. This program or assessment is used across the United States in numerous capacities and is norm-referenced. As Mastery was in full swing in Mezinko's class we were excited to see the RIT growth by winter. When the winter assessments from NWEA were completed by the students, the gap started to widen. Mezinko average RIT score was 197 with a standard deviation of 8.5 and the non-mastery group was 190 with a standard deviation of 10.87. As we know through Hattie's research, every type of instruction works, however, using higher effect size strategies increase student achievement at a greater pace. The students took the spring assessment with only about 6 weeks of instruction after the winter assessment due to holiday breaks, etc. Mezinko's class had an average RIT score of 199 and a standard deviation of 6.5. The non-mastery class had a RIT score of 190 with a standard deviation of 7.2. Using statistical practices, I knew that the lower the standard deviation, the more accurate the data set. However, I expected high standard deviation due to the small sample size. The deviations between the two classrooms were close, however, the RIT scores had increased significantly in Mezinko's classroom. This was starting to show on a summative basis that the Instructional Model of Math Mastery-Based Learning Initiative IM^3 was working. Our results on the formative basis confirmed that the math mastery process was improving student performance. The summative assessments that were completed confirmed the growth that the formative data showed on an ongoing basis. The results were being validated! We knew we had changed the paradigm of math instruction at our school.

When the results for the Ohio State Assessments came out, our determination to scale this IM^3 initiative grew even more. We knew we had broken part of the barrier between urban education and growth. Below are the results over a three-year period for the entire school:

Year over Year Comparison of 3rd Grade Ohio State Testing Results

Year	School	Chase %	District %	State %	Mastery Level Began	+/- District
15-16	Chase	17.6%	32.2%	54.9%	no	-14.6
16-17	Chase	17.1%	40.1%	63.8%	no/partial	-22.9
17-18	Chase	68%	41.4%	67%	Yes	+26%

Gap Closing Data

One of the most important pieces of being in an Urban environment is ensuring minority students show growth at the same level as other students. Our most recent State Report Card showed that we scored a perfect 100% in math. In other words, every minority student grew at a rate higher than anticipated in all tested grades.

The graphic on the following page is taken from the State of Ohio's Report Card System. This is from summative data following the 2017 school year. This information shows how the various subgroups of our school made drastic improvements in math achievement. Specific focus on minority and students with disabilities demonstrates how this instructional model of Math Mastery-Based Mathematics IM^3 works in urban environments. Every student in Mezinko's class not only scored proficient, they scored above proficient. This equates to all of her learners growing more than one year's growth in one year's time. On the following page is a breakdown of the performance index for each subgroup in our school. Performance index is based out of 100 percentage points.

AMO - Math Proficiency

Subgroup	Metrics Took Test #	Perf Index	Goal	LT Goal	LT Gap	Took Test LY #	Perf Index LY	Improve	LT Gap Close %	VA Gain Index	Points
All Students	200	79.150	84.2	100.0	20.9	183	56.885	22.3	106.8	9.8	100.0
Am. Indian or Alaskan Native	2	NC	76.8	87.1	NC	0	NC	NC	NC	0.0	NR
Asian or Pacific Islander	0	NC	97.8	98.8	NC	0	NC	NC	NC	0.0	NR
Black, Non-Hispanic	109	79.083	61.3	78.5	N/A	108	52.222	N/A	N/A	7.5	100.0
Hispanic	19	NC	72.3	84.6	NC	11	NC	NC	NC	3.6	NR
Multiracial	34	80.588	77.7	87.6	N/A	26	60.385	N/A	N/A	3.9	100.0
White, Non-Hispanic	36	72.222	87.6	93.1	20.9	38	64.737	7.5	35.9	1.8	100.0
Economic Disadvantage	200	79.150	71.1	84.0	N/A	183	56.885	N/A	N/A	9.8	100.0
English Learner	2	NC	70.1	83.4	NC	0	NC	NC	NC	0.0	NR
Students with Disabilities	54	58.333	56.2	76.8	N/A	52	33.077	N/A	N/A	4.3	100.0

Total of Subgroup Points: 600.0
Possible Subgroup Points: 600.0
Math Points Earned (Total / Possible): 100.0

Below is the data from the State of Ohio Report Card for my school from the 2016 school year. This data is not specific to Mezinko, however as we know, the top 20% of an organization is responsible for 80% of the growth.

White	Economically Disadvantaged	African American	Students with Disabilities
39.5%	28.6%	22.4%	2%

"We knew if we focused on student growth as our "one thing", we would be amazed at the results!

Summary of Evidence

"I hated every minute of training, but I said don't quit. Suffer now and live the rest of your life as a champion"

Muhammed Ali

I was told an old Native American Tale by a retired US Marine. He told the story to me and I will never forget it. He stated "Tell your child or children they each have two wolves inside of them. One is a vicious and competitive wolf and the other a kind and loving wolf. The wolves inside are constantly battling. He said that kids would ask him which one wins? His response was "the one you feed." This story resonated with me while I was reflecting on the work we decided to put into this math initiative. We could have fed the vicious wolf and used archaic traditional methods or we could've looked at each individual student and worked toward mastery with them. We chose to feed the caring wolf as the mantra of which wolf we wanted to feed at our school.

Using the instructional model of mastery learning in mathematics, IM^3, has changed the culture of instruction in our building. No longer are we guessing which instructional strategy to use, we know which strategies have the greatest effect size for our demographics. We know the importance of mastery, as it is the one item that can ensure transfer occurs at the cognitive level. Judy Willis, MD, states "It is important to evaluate and plan so that each student works at an individually appropriate level of achievable challenge." By using a mastery chart, we know which students are struggling with each standard. This allows the educator and other stakeholders to use an intervention strategy to help the learner improve the area where they have not reached mastery.

Summary

Ron Clark states "You can spend your time at school however you choose, but you can only spend it once." When Clark spoke those words to a group of us, it resonated with me that each day we have to ensure we are moving our learners toward the goal of more than one year's growth in one year's time. The Navigators, Aspiring Navigators and Riders, with some coaching and support, all have the same mentality each day they enter our building.

Through my own research and reading numerous books, Simon Sinek's quote resonated with me, as a leader, still to this day, years after reading his work. "If a movement is to have an impact it must belong to those who join it not just those who lead it." **Mastery truly is a self-driven process.** Educators choose to lead autonomously and work toward their students mastering the concepts at their own pace while understanding each other's purpose. The purpose of the educator is to relate the learning to how it will improve the lives of their students. The students' role is to own the mastery process knowing they each have the same purpose.

The purpose of this instructional model IM^3 is to create mastery in mathematics for all learners to grow more than one year's growth in one year's time!

Backstory on the Authors

Jack Hunter

As author and principal I want to share my backstory with you. My mother, who I owe my entire educational journey to, was an urban teacher and focused on empowering urban children to reach their potential. Visiting my mother's classroom and attending a very diverse high school in urban Cleveland provided a passage to my journey as an educator. I remember driving down to 41st street in Cleveland, Oh and visiting the school where she taught. As I walked down the hallway to my mother's classroom, I peered in the other classrooms. Students were actively engaged in learning and teachers were sharing their excitement in teaching. Seeing and most importantly hearing the student conversations that were taking place around subject content, further compelled me to follow my mother's career path. Her school was a Blue Ribbon School and one in which the leader had a steadfast approach to learning and how she approached the learning process with her staff members. Watching my mom prepare lessons and spend hours after school preparing her room, showed me that teaching was a calling not a career. This became the platform for the start of my educational journey. I grew up in middle class Cleveland, OH and attended a very diverse Cleveland High School. I graduated from The University of Toledo with a focus in math education and immediately accepted a position in urban Toledo at a high poverty school in a high crime area. The commitment that it would take to show student growth, as well as, creating an innovative classroom was my vision of what an educator does. Educators who have the passion to teach run to the area where the children need dedicated vested instructors the most. My first year I was a math specialist and quickly helped change the culture of math education in the school. When I would enter the room the students would look at the activities I planned for that lesson and I would hear comments such as, "where are the worksheets?" Students would say the only time we have fun in math is when we play "Quizmo" Bingo. This compelled me to spend even more time planning engaging differentiated lessons even though I only had the students once or twice a week for one hour blocks. To me that was enough time to improve their perception of being an astute math student and creating a mindset of an appreciation of the importance of mathematics. I was fortunate enough to find and use some really innovative NCTM (National Council for Teachers of Mathematics) publications that had some pre-made engaging lessons. I used this as a starting point for the standards and then let my passion create the environment for success. Promoting that we learn by understanding and correcting our mistakes is not an easy thing to delve into with urban children. The students I instructed were extremely resilient and witty, however, they had become accustomed to our archaic grading practices which did not benefit students who were trying to stretch their minds. The system benefited the students who could sit and regurgitate the content. After completing the year I became even more eager to lead my own classroom and decided that I needed to instruct in an area where there is an extreme shortage of qualified math instructors. I decided to move and accept a job in inner-city Detroit at a high turnover, 100% free reduced lunch school. This was where I would find out if I really wanted to be in urban education.

Abbey Mezinko

As an author and teacher I truly believe I am following the career path I was called to do. I grew up in a middle class family in Toledo, Ohio. I attended Toledo Public Schools and always enjoyed my educational experiences. As a child, I had a classroom that my father set up for me in my basement. I remember spending hours playing "school" where I always insisted on being the teacher. I would be down there every evening, weekend and summer. I remember my parents yelling at me to come up for dinner. I just couldn't stop making worksheets or grading my friend's tests I would give them.

My aunt was a teacher in The Toledo Public School District and I would spend many weekends and summers visiting her classroom and helping her set up for the beginning of the school year. I remember passing out textbooks and stacking them neatly on every student's desk. I felt such joy when the classroom would be complete and ready for students. I always enjoyed listening to my aunt's stories about her students and the different lessons she would have planned for them. These trips always made me eager to have a classroom I could one day call my own. There was never a doubt in my mind that teaching would always be my life. I always excelled in school and stayed focused on achieving the personal goals I had set for myself to ensure I would succeed.

I chose to stay close to home for college as I attended The University of Toledo, majoring in Early Childhood Education. Following college, I couldn't have been happier when I was offered a job in the district I grew up attending. This career has brought me so much happiness and has given me the drive to continue learning professionally to better the educational experiences of my learners.

I am eager to begin my fifth year teaching. The school that I have been blessed to teach at is in an inner city Toledo neighborhood. This school is in an area completely different than where I grew up. I was very out of my element when I began teaching here, but since starting, I have realized how important the relationships are that I strive to build with my students. The daily struggles they face are more than I could ever imagine being challenged with at their young age. My passion for teaching has grown more every year as I watch my students strive to reach success. I work for a Principal who motivates teachers, staff and students daily and gives every child the opportunity to become the best that they can be. I have learned how to not only educate my learners, but to also support each student and give them confidence. From all this, I have learned that despite my student's daily challenges outside of the classroom, they still show the ability and the drive to learn.

My goal is to continue to educate my learners and give them an education they deserve. I hope they can learn to love their education and value it. My teaching can change their lives and help them become successful in their future aspirations.

Additional Mastery Problems
I would recommend solving these two questions in a PLC or staff meeting

When working with a larger number of students and modeling how you should work in groups and problem solve together, I provide questions that are open ended and lead to more questions. An example of a question is:

Twenty-five people attend a party. If each person shakes hands with every other person at the party, how many handshakes will there be?

A simple question that would seem surface level can lead to deep discussion amongst students. I normally will model this by having 25 students come to the front and demonstrate solving this problem. It builds up perseverance and also allows students to understand that problem solving is all just understanding information.

Another example: I post to staff and students when modeling perseverance and real world application is:

You are driving your Porsche and see that your tank of gas is only 3/8 full. The tank holds 14 gallons of gas. Your Porsche gets 18 ½ miles for every gallon of gas. How far can you drive before you run out of gas? What factors might contribute to the 18 ½ going up or down and why?

This is a multi-step problem that fits multiple standards and standards for mathematical practice.

Sample Mastery Level Problems

What Mastery Level would this question be and why? (Answer this question for all the applicable problems)

Question #1   Kindergarten Problem

Have the class line up and give directions to the student assessed to position him/herself in the line according to the ordinal number that you give. i.e stand 8th in line. Or stand 2 spots behind student A.

What Mastery Level would this question be and why? (Answer this question for all the applicable problems)

Question #2   Kindergarten Problem

Have an individual student count to 100

Question #3   Kindergarten Problem

Give the tested student a variety of items to use and ask him/her to measure objects and compare larger to smaller and why?

Question #4   1st Grade Problem

Show all the different ways to make combinations of six. Draw models to represent your strategy

Question # 5   1ˢᵗ Grade Problem

Survey the class and find out how many students rode the bus to school. Then determine how many students could have walked or been driven to school. List and explain the different possibilities with a classmate.

Question #6   1ˢᵗ Grade Problem

There were 8 apples in a picnic basket. John ate 2 apples. Sue ate 3 apples. How many apples are left?

Question #7   2ⁿᵈ Grade Problem

If you have 1quarter, 5 dimes, 2 nickels and 4 pennies, how many cents do you have?

Question #8   2ⁿᵈ Grade Problem

Make 83 cents in two different ways with either quarters, nickels, dimes or pennies.

Question #9   2ⁿᵈ Grade Problem

Make 72 cents using exactly 9 coins that are either quarters, dimes, nickels or pennies.

Question #10   3ʳᵈ Grade Problem

$821 - 357 =$

Question #11   3rd Grade Problem

Use the digits 1 to 9, at most one time each, to fill in the boxes to make a difference that is as close to 329 as possible.

___ ___ ___ − ___ ___ ___ =

Question #12   3rd Grade Problem

Using the whole numbers 1 through 9 as numerators or denominators, how many fractions can you make that are less than one half?

Question #13 Accelerated Class   4th Grade Problem

Jayla subtracted 7/12 - 1/2 and found a difference of 6/10.

Ask the students to use what they know about fractions to explain why you agree or disagree with Jayla. Use models, numbers, or words to explain your thinking.

(The whole purpose of this problem is to provoke the misunderstanding of when students subtract denominators from denominators and numerators from numerators. This will help you evaluate if a child has mastered the concept not just a shortcut.)

Question #14   4th Grade Problem

Mrs. Mezinko has some stickers. When she gives 4 stickers or 5 stickers to each student, she has 2 stickers left. There are no stickers left when she gives 6 stickers to each student. What is the least number of stickers Mrs. Mezinko could have?

Question #15   4th Grade Problem

Place a < **or** > between the two fractions to make a true number sentence.

$$\frac{3}{8} \qquad \frac{2}{3}$$

Question #16   5th Grade Problem

Max has $150. He spends $68 on pants and $59 on sandals. Does he have enough money to buy a $35 tee shirt?

Question #17   5th Grade Problem

Lilly works a total of 16 hours on Friday, Saturday and Sunday. She works twice as many hours on Saturday as Friday. Lilly works 4 hours on Sunday. How many hours does Lilly work on Saturday?

Question #18   5th Grade Problem

Tyrone is sure that when you divide with fractions, you get smaller numbers. In class, his group divides $4 \div 1/3$ and gets 12. Tyrone disagrees with his group. Do you agree with Tyrone or his group? Use models, numbers or words to explain your thinking.

(So many students believe that when you divide by a fraction you will always get smaller number. This above problem creates learning opportunities and also a way to create a model to prove it. Using a model to show how many 1/3 are in 1 and how many 1/3 are in 2 is paramount for the students to understand this problem.)

Question #19   6th Grade Problem

A restaurant worker used 5 loaves of wheat bread and 2 loaves of rye bread to make sandwiches for an event.

Write a ratio that compares the number of loaves of rye bread to the number of loaves of wheat bread.

Describe what the ratio

7:2 means in terms of the loaves of bread used for the event.

Question #20   6th Grade Problem

Ben's Game World is having a sale on video games.
The store is offering a sale pack of 4 video games for $43.80. What is the unit price of a video game in the sale pack?

$ _____

Roberto's Electronics is also having a sale on video games. The unit price of any video game at Roberto's Electronics is the same as the unit price of a video game in the sale pack at Ben's Game World. How much would it cost a customer for 7 video games at Roberto's Electronics?

$ _____

Question #21   6th Grade Problem

For numbers 1a-1c, select Yes or No to indicate whether the pairs are equivalent expressions.

1a. Are $4(3x - y)$ and $12x - 4y$ equivalent expressions?

Yes   No

1b. Are $32 + 16y$ and $8(4 + 2y)$ equivalent expressions?

Yes   No

1c. Are $3(x + 2y)$ and $3x + 2y$ equivalent expressions?

Yes   No

Question #22   7th Grade Problem

Renee, Susan, and Martha will share the cost to rent a vacation house for a week.

- Renee will pay 40% of the cost.
- Susan will pay 0.35 of the cost.
- Martha will pay the remainder of the cost.

Part A

Martha thinks that she will pay $\frac{1}{3}$ of the cost. Is Martha correct? Use mathematics to justify your answer.

Part B

The cost to rent a vacation house for a week is $850. How much will Renee, Susan, and Martha each pay to rent this house for a week?

Renee will pay $ [   ]

Susan will pay $ [   ]

Martha will pay $ [   ]

Question #23   7th Grade Problem

In the following equation, a and b are both integers.

$$a(3x - 8) = (b - 18x)$$

What is the value of a? _____

What is the value of b? _____

Question #24   7th Grade Problem

Consider a circle that has a circumference of 28π centimeters (cm).

Part A
What is the area, in cm2, of this circle? Show all work necessary to justify your response.

Part B
What would be the measure of the radius, in cm, of a circle with an area that is 20% greater than the circle in Part A?

Show all work necessary to justify your response

Question #25   8th Grade Problem

Fill in each x-value and y-value in the table below to create a relation that is **not** a function.

X	Y

Question #26   8th Grade Problem

Juan needs a right cylindrical storage tank that holds between 110 and 115 cubic feet
of water.
Using whole numbers only, provide the radius and height for 3 different tanks that hold between 110 and 115 cubic feet of water.

Tank #1   radius=_____ ft.
                   height=_____ ft.

Tank #2   radius=_____ ft.
                   height=_____ ft.

Tank #3   radius=_____ ft.
                   height=_____ ft.

Question #27   **8th Grade Math Problem**

3908 Nyx is an asteroid between Mars and Jupiter. Let d represent the approximate distance from 3908 Nyx to the Sun.
The average distance from Venus to the Sun is about (7×10^7) miles.
The average distance from Jupiter to the Sun is about (5×10^8) miles.

At a certain time of year, the square distance from 3908 Nyx to the Sun is equal to the product of the average distance from Venus to the Sun and the average distance from Jupiter to the Sun. This equation can be used to find the distance from 3908 Nyx to the Sun, d, at this time of year.

$$d^2 = (7 \times 10^7)(5 \times 10^8)$$

Solve the equation for d. Round your answer to the nearest million.
d = _____ miles

Answer Key

We specifically selected more level 2 problems as the majority of the problems on Standardized tests are level 2 (66%). Level One are normally the straight algorithmic problems in text books.

Question A	**64 Stamps; Mastery Level 2**	
Question B	**Mastery Level 3**	
Question C	**Mastery Level 2**	
Question D	**Mastery Level 2**	$\left(3\frac{4}{6} - 2\frac{3}{6} = 1\frac{1}{6}\right)$
Question E	**Mastery Level 2 or 3**	
Question F	**Mastery Level 2 or 3**	
Question #1	**Mastery Level 3**	
Question #2	**Mastery Level 1**	
Question #3	**Mastery Level 2 or 3**	
Question # 4	**Mastery Level 2**	
Question # 5	**Mastery Level 3**	
Question #6	**Mastery Level 2**	
Question #7	**Mastery Level 1**	
Questions #8	**Mastery Level 2**	
Question #9	**Mastery Level 3**	
Question #10	**Mastery Level 1**	
Question #11	**Mastery Level 3**	
Question #12	**Mastery Level 2**	
Question #13	**Mastery Level 3**	
Question #14	**Mastery Level 3 or Accelerated**	
Question # 15	**Mastery Level 1**	
Question #16	**Mastery Level 2**	

Question #17   Mastery Level 3 or Accelerated

Question #18   Mastery Level 2 or 3

Question #19   Mastery Level 2

(2:5 part one
7:2 is the ratio of the total number of loaves of bread to the number of loaves of rye bread)

Question #20   Mastery Level 2

($10.95 ; $76.65)

Question #21   Mastery Level 1
(YYN)

Question #22   Mastery Level 2

Part A
Martha is incorrect. She will pay 1/4 of the cost.

$1 - (40\% + 0.35)$
$1 - (0.40 + 0.35)$
$1 - 0.75$
$0.25 = \dfrac{25}{100} = \dfrac{1}{4}$

Part B
Renee - $340
Susan - $297.50
Martha - $212.50

Question #23   Mastery Level 2

(a. -6 b. 48)

Questions #24   Mastery Level 3

Part A

First, I found the radius: $r = \frac{28\pi}{2\pi} = 14$ cm. Then I found the area:
$A = \pi(14^2) = 196\pi$ cm². **OR** $A \approx (3.14)(14^2) \approx 615.44$ cm².

Part B

First, I multiplied the area of the circle in Part A by 1.20 (which is 20% more than the original): $A = 196\pi(1.20) = 235.2\pi$ cm². Then I found the radius by solving the area formula for r:
$$235.2\pi = \pi r^2$$
$$235.2 = r^2$$
$$15.34 \approx r$$

Question # 25   Mastery Level 1

The purpose of the item is to determine whether students understand that a function assigns exactly one output to each input in its domain. This is an example of a level 1 problem. Sample answer:

X	Y
4	0
4	1
4	2
4	3
4	4

Question #26   **Mastery Level 2 or 3**

Sample Answers:

Tank #1 r=2; h=9

Tank #2 r=3; h=4

Tank #3 r= 6; h=1

Students must have a thorough understanding of volume of cylinders

This is a Level 2 or 3 based upon depth of instruction

Question # 27   **Mastery Level 2**

(Answer: 187,000,000)

Notes

Ship Bound to Mastery Island

We wish you great success on your journey to Math Mastery using the IM^3 Model.

Jack & Abbey

Works Cited

Clifton, Don. Strengths finder 2.0: Discover your Clifton Strengths. Gallup Press 2007

Hattie, John A. C. *Visible Learning: a Synthesis of over 800 Meta-Analyses Relating to Achievement*. Routledge, 2009.

Keller, Gary. *The One Thing: The Surprisingly Simple Truth Behind Extraordinary Results. Bard Press, 2012.*

Leinwand, Steven. *Accessible Mathematics: 10 Instructional Shifts Thats Raise Student Achievement.* Heinemann, 2009.

Muhammed, Anthony. *Transforming School Culture: How To Overcome Staff Division. Solution Tree Press, 2009.*

Pink, Daniel. Drive: *The Surprising Truth About What Motivates Us.* Riverhead Books, 2011.

Sinek, Simon. *Start With Why: How Great Leaders inspire Everyone To Take Action. Penguin 2009*

Small, Marian. *Uncomplicating Fractions: To Meet Common Core Standards in Math, K-7. Teachers College Press, 2014.*

Willis, Judy M.D. *Learning to Love Math: Teaching strategies that change student attitudes and get results.* ASCD, 2010.

Some sample problems taken from released smarter balanced tests and Robert Kaplinksy.com

Made in the USA
San Bernardino, CA
31 July 2019